Sams **Teach Yourself**

Google
Voice

in **10 Minutes**

800 East 96th Street, Indianapolis, Indiana 46240

ISBN-13: 978-0-672-33308-8
ISBN-10: 0-672-33308-2

Library of Congress Cataloging-in-Publication Data is on file.

Printed in the United States on America

First Printing May 2010

Trademarks

All terms mentioned in this book that are known to be trademarks or service marks have been appropriately capitalized. Sams Publishing cannot attest to the accuracy of this information. Use of a term in this book should not be regarded as affecting the validity of any trademark or service mark.

Warning and Disclaimer

Every effort has been made to make this book as complete and as accurate as possible, but no warranty or fitness is implied. The information provided is on an "as is" basis. The author and the publisher shall have neither liability nor responsibility to any person or entity with respect to any loss or damages arising from the information contained in this book.

Bulk Sales

Sams Publishing offers excellent discounts on this book when ordered in quantity for bulk purchases or special sales. For more information, please contact

U.S. Corporate and Government Sales

1-800-382-3419

corpsales@pearsontechgroup.com

For sales outside of the U.S., please contact

International Sales

international@pearsoned.com

Associate Publisher
Greg Wiegand

Acquisitions Editor
Michelle Newcomb

Development Editor
Charlotte Kughen

Managing Editor
Sandra Schroeder

Project Editor
Seth Kerney

Copy Editor
Language Logistics

Indexer
Erika Millen

Proofreader
Dan Knott

Technical Editor
Christian Kenyeres

Publishing Coordinator
Cindy Teeters

Designer
Gary Adair

Contents

About the Author

Nancy Conner writes and edits technology books from her home in central New York state. Her recent publications include books on Google Docs and Google Apps. Nancy has also worked as a medievalist, a high school teacher, and a corporate trainer. She enjoys reading mystery novels and listening obsessively to opera.

Dedication

To Steve (and he knows exactly why).

Acknowledgments

The book you're holding is the result of many people's hard work. Thanks to Michelle Newcomb for discussing the original idea for this book and keeping me on track throughout its writing. Thanks also to Charlotte Kughen for guidance as I wrote, to Christian Kenyeres for a conscientious and thorough technical review, and to Chrissy White for making sure all my i's were dotted and t's crossed. Seth Kerney did a terrific job of overseeing the process of turning a manuscript into a book.

We Want to Hear from You!

As the reader of this book, *you* are our most important critic and commentator. We value your opinion and want to know what we're doing right, what we could do better, what areas you'd like to see us publish in, and any other words of wisdom you're willing to pass our way.

As an associate publisher for Sams Publishing, I welcome your comments. You can email or write me directly to let me know what you did or didn't like about this book—as well as what we can do to make our books better.

Please note that I cannot help you with technical problems related to the topic of this book. We do have a User Services group, however, where I will forward specific technical questions related to the book.

When you write, please be sure to include this book's title and author as well as your name, email address, and phone number. I will carefully review your comments and share them with the author and editors who worked on the book.

Email: consumer@samspublishing.com

Mail: Greg Wiegand
          Associate Publisher
          Sams Publishing
          800 East 96th Street
          Indianapolis, IN 46240 USA

Reader Services

Visit our website and register this book at www.samspublishing.com/register for convenient access to any updates, downloads, or errata that might be available for this book.

Introduction

Welcome to Google Voice, your complete phone management system.

Google Voice lets you manage incoming calls—specifying where to send them (you can ring up to six phones for a single incoming call)—and make free calls in the United States and Canada (and very cheap international calls). But that's just the beginning of this feature-rich system.

Google Voice has dozens of features, which is terrific if you've got serious phone requirements, but you shouldn't let all of those features intimidate you if your needs are more limited. Google Voice provides you with a smorgasbord of choices, but you can start with the most popular and then dig into what else is available when you have time.

What's in This Book

This book gives you a guided tour of Google Voice, from setting up to making and receiving calls to using advanced features like call forwarding and custom voicemail greetings. You see what's available in Google Voice so that you can make choices about what you want and need.

Google Voice offers you tons of options, which are all covered in this book:

- ▶ Making calls (for free in the U.S. and Canada)
- ▶ Getting voicemail alerts sent to your mobile phone
- ▶ Forwarding calls to up to six phones
- ▶ Reading transcripts of your voicemails
- ▶ Getting a free Google phone number
- ▶ Storing contact information
- ▶ Listening as people record voicemail for you
- ▶ Making inexpensive international calls

- ▶ Using one voicemail greeting for some people and a different greeting for others

- ▶ Screening calls by having Google Voice ask for the callers' names before passing the calls on to you

- ▶ Sending and receiving free text messages

And there's even more to learn as we drill down into more detailed topics (such as temporary call forwarding). All in all, you'll get the whole Google Voice story.

What You'll Need

You don't need much to work with Google Voice—just a phone (which can be a mobile phone) and a computer that can connect to the Google Voice website. We'll go over system requirements in more detail in Lesson 1, "Welcome to Google Voice," but Google Voice officially supports Windows XP, Windows Vista, Mac OS X, and Linux.

What's missing from that list? Windows 7. At this writing, Google Voice doesn't currently list Windows 7 as being officially supported by Google Voice. On the other hand, we've tested and all seems fine—we had no problems using Google Voice with Windows 7.

Choose a Web Browser

To use Google Voice, you need a web browser—you can pick from one of these:

- ▶ IE6 and above

- ▶ Firefox 3 and above

- ▶ Safari 3 and above

- ▶ Google Chrome

> NOTE
> Your browser needs to support Flash 8 (or later) to work with Google Voice.

Get an Invitation

As of this writing there's one more thing you need to get started with Google Voice—an invitation from Google. Currently, you must be invited to join Google Voice—either by Google or by someone who already has a Google Voice account—to use the service. There's no official word yet about when Google Voice will be open to everyone.

We go through this in more detail and see how to request an invitation from Google Voice in Lesson 2, "Signing up and Getting Started," which is all about actually signing up and signing in with Google Voice.

> TIP
> Invitations that come directly from Google take a lot longer than invitations from people who already use Google Voice; the latter are immediate. So if you have a pal who uses Google Voice, see if you can get an invitation through him.

Of course at some point, Google will no longer require invitations to set up a Google Voice account. In fact, invitations may no longer be required by the time you read this. You see how to tell whether or not invitations are needed in Lesson 2.

Conventions Used in This Book

In the step-by-step instructions in this book, anything you need to click, press, or type is in **bold** text, such as "Click the **Settings** link to open the Settings page."

We've also included some special sidebars that call out information that is of special interest.

> NOTE
> Notes include extra information that might give you a deeper understanding of a topic and that help you expand your knowledge.

> **TIP**
>
> Tips offer suggestions for getting things done more quickly or easily.

> **CAUTION**
>
> Cautions are warnings that alert you to possible consequences or an outcome of using a particular task or feature.

> **PLAIN ENGLISH**
>
> Plain English sidebars define acronyms or jargon that you might not already know.

Where to Go From Here

All right—we're ready to begin. First, let's orient ourselves in Google Voice and see what it has to offer with an overview in Lesson 1.

Then we discuss how to sign up and sign in to Google Voice in Lesson 2, which is all about getting started. You will get signed up with Google Voice and be ready to go.

Lesson 3, "Making a Call," is all about, guess what, making calls, while Lesson 4, "Answering a Call," is all about getting them. By the end of Lesson 4 we'll be well and truly launched into Google Voice, and you will have the basics down. The rest of the book is devoted to mastering Google Voice's many cool features.

Let's start now: Turn the page to Lesson 1, which gives you a 10,000-foot view of Google Voice and what it can do for you.

Welcome to Google Voice

People are buzzing about Google Voice. You may have heard about it in the news, on your favorite tech blog, or on social networking sites like Twitter or Facebook. What's so great about Google Voice?

That's the question we answer in this lesson. Here, you'll get a guided tour of what Google Voice is about and all it has to offer.

Let's get started.

What's in Google Voice?

Google Voice is a complete telephone management system. Here's a sampling of what you can do with it:

- ▶ Get your own free Google phone number (or use an existing mobile phone number).
- ▶ Make free calls to people in the U.S. and Canada.
- ▶ Receive calls.
- ▶ Screen calls.
- ▶ Forward calls.
- ▶ Get written transcriptions of your voicemails.
- ▶ Be alerted on your mobile phone when you've got voicemail waiting.
- ▶ Keep track of your contacts (and call them with a click).
- ▶ Listen in as someone records a voicemail message for you.
- ▶ Send and receive text messages.

▶ Play one voicemail greeting for one group of people and a different greeting for another group.

▶ Make inexpensive international calls.

▶ Set up temporary call forwarding from any phone.

▶ Place call widgets on a web page so people looking at your page can call you with just a click.

▶ Much, much more.

This lesson gives you an overview of Google Voice's features so you can orient yourself. Knowing what Google Voice offers is essential for using it effectively.

So what does Google Voice look like? Take a look at Figure 1.1, which shows the page you see after you've logged in to Google Voice.

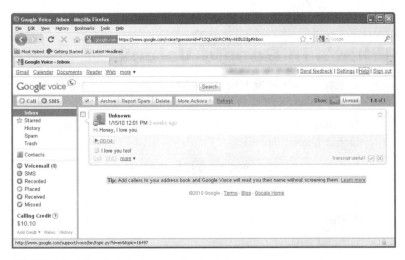

FIGURE 1.1   The Google Voice call center.

This is your call center—the place where you manage all your calls. The center pane of the Google Voice page is where the action is. That's where you see transcriptions of voicemails, your text messages, and your contacts, as well as manage your settings.

At the top of the page, you see a toolbar that includes buttons such as Call and SMS. The Call button lets you place a call through Google Voice (read Lesson 3, "Making a Call," for more information about how it works). The SMS button lets you send text messages, and composing text messages at your computer's keyboard is a heck of a lot easier than doing so on a mobile phone's keypad.

Below the toolbar on the left is a set of links, such as

- ▶ Inbox
- ▶ Starred
- ▶ History
- ▶ Spam
- ▶ Trash
- ▶ Contacts
- ▶ Voicemail
- ▶ SMS

Those links are how you manage Google Voice. When you click the Inbox link, for example, the center pane shows you a list of the text messages you've received and the transcriptions of your voicemails. (Google Voice actually converts spoken voicemails into text—read Lesson 5, "Using Voicemail," to learn more about the voicemail options in Google Voice.) When you click the SMS button, only your text messages appear in the center pane. When you click the Contacts link, your address book appears, and you can call any contact with just a click.

The Settings page, which you access by clicking the Settings link in the main page, and which appears in Figure 1.2, lets you configure Google Voice preferences.

The Settings page contains seven tabs, as you can see in the figure. Here's an overview:

- ▶ **Phones:** Lets you tell Google Voice about your phones so you can use Google Voice with those phones.

- ▶ **Voicemail & SMS:** Lets you specify who gets a voicemail greeting and who doesn't and also sets other voicemail and text message options (such as forwarding text messages to an email account).

FIGURE 1.2   The Settings page.

▶ **Calls:** Lets you specify whether or not you want caller ID, lets you turn off all calls with a Do Not Disturb setting, and more.

▶ **Groups:** Lets you gather contacts into related groups and specify options, such as voicemail options, for those groups—so, for example, work contacts could get one voicemail greeting and family another.

▶ **Call Widgets:** Keeps track of the snippets of HTML code you've created that you can embed in a web page to let people call you with a single click.

▶ **Billing:** Keeps track of what you've been billed for, such as international calls.

▶ **Account:** Lets you specify the credit card you want Google Voice to use for billable items.

NOTE

Billing? Account? Don't worry, most of what you'll do with Google Voice is free. There is a charge for making an international call, but it's not much compared to most other calling plans.

That's an overview of the Google Voice interface. Now let's go under the hood to take a look at some of the best features Google Voice offers.

Managing Multiple Phones

Perhaps the most popular reason for using Google Voice is that it lets you manage multiple phones.

Say that you have three different phones on which people can reach you—at home, at the office, and at your parents' house. In that case, you could get a free Google Voice number (or use an existing mobile phone number) so that when people call that number, all three of those phones ring.

You can set this up in the Phones tab of the Settings page, as you can see in Figure 1.2, where you list the numbers your Google phone number forwards to.

Setting up a single Google Voice number that people can use to call you means that people only need to remember one number for you. Even when you move, you can just forward calls to your new landline if you use one.

In addition, you can customize Google Voice's behavior for different callers, sending some callers directly to voicemail, for example, and others directly to you. In this way, Google Voice can act as your answering service, sending the calls you want straight to you and taking a message otherwise.

Screening Calls

Another way Google Voice can act as your answering service is by screening your calls. You can set things up so that when someone calls your Google Voice number, he or she is asked to provide a name, which Google Voice records. Google Voice then calls you and gives the person's name, giving you the option of taking the call or sending it to voicemail.

This feature is called *Call Presentation.* If you have Call Presentation turned on, Google asks callers for their names and relays the names to you. If you've turned off Call Presentation, Google Voice acts like a normal telephone, without asking callers for their names.

You turn Call Presentation on or off in the Calls tab of the Settings page, as you see in Figure 1.3. (Lesson 4, "Answering a Call," tells you more about Call Presentation.)

FIGURE 1.3   Turning Call Presentation on and off.

Making Calls

Besides receiving calls, Google Voice is also an expert at letting you make calls.

You can make calls from any phone by calling your Google Voice number and following the prompts, or you can click the Call button on the Google Voice website.

When you click the Call button, a drop-down box appears, as you see in Figure 1.4.

FIGURE 1.4   Making a call.

In the drop-down box, you just enter the number to call (domestic or international), select a phone for Google Voice to call you on (it will call you first and then place the call and connect you), and click the Connect button. Lesson 3 spells out the details.

Calls to the U.S. and Canada are free, and international calls are very cheap—typically one-fifth (or less) of what your phone company charges.

Voicemail Transcriptions

Google Voice is packed with cool features, and one of the coolest is voice-mail transcriptions. When Google Voice takes a message for you, it records the caller's voice (and lets you play back the message with a click), but it also converts the spoken message into text.

You can see a sample transcription in the Inbox shown in Figure 1.1. How good is the transcription process? Surprisingly good, it turns out, even with proper names and long words. (If Google Voice isn't sure about a particular word, it displays that word in light-colored text.)

Getting transcriptions of your voicemail means you can search your voicemails by specifying a word or term to search for, which is very cool. It also means that you can get your voicemails in email if you like.

It's also worth noting that, as with just about all Google Voice features, if you don't like this feature, you can turn it off.

Advanced Voicemail for an Existing Mobile Number

You can set up Google Voice so that you get a new phone number assigned by Google Voice. But if you'd rather not change your phone number, you can also set up Google Voice to use an existing mobile phone number (not a landline).

What that means in a nutshell is that you can convert your mobile phone into a Google Voice phone. For most of the larger carriers, Google Voice will actually take over the voicemail system of your mobile phone.

In other words, when a caller leaves a voicemail on your mobile phone, the caller goes through the Google Voice system, not, say, AT&T's or Verizon's voicemail system. Lesson 4 covers which carriers let you replace their voicemail system with the Google Voice voicemail system.

Keep Track of Your Contacts

Does Google Voice let you keep a phone book of people you routinely call? Yes, it does. They're called *contacts*, and you can see the contacts you've set up by clicking the left-hand Contacts link on any Google Voice page. A sample Contacts page is shown in Figure 1.5.

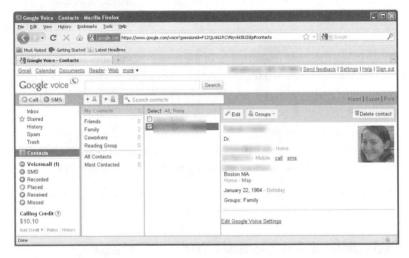

FIGURE 1.5   A Contacts page.

You can call or text any contact simply by opening that contact's page and clicking the call or SMS link.

A Contacts page is about more than easy calling or texting, however—setting up a page for a contact tells Google Voice about that person. When someone is a Google Voice contact, here's what you can do:

- ▶ Always send calls from that person to voicemail.

- ▶ Add that person to a group.

- ▶ Select the voicemail greeting the person gets.

- ▶ Block calls from that person.

Listen in As a Caller Records Voicemail

Here's another cool feature—you can eavesdrop as a caller records a voicemail message for you.

Undoubtedly, Google Voice was inspired by answering machines on this feature. With an answering machine, you can listen in as someone leaves a message—picking up if the call is interesting or letting the machine record the message otherwise.

Google Voice works similarly. When someone calls your Google Voice number and you've got Call Presentation turned on, Google Voice then calls you to give you the name of the person who's calling—and you have the option of sending the caller to voicemail while you listen in on the message.

If the message turns out to be something you want to talk about, you can break in and start talking with the caller—just as you could with an answering machine. Try doing that with regular voicemail!

Inexpensive International Calling

Domestic calls have been getting cheaper and cheaper, but international rates are still often sky-high (although they're coming down for some carriers), especially when you call from your mobile phone.

If you're tired of spending a lot on international calls, Google Voice has a solution—inexpensive international calling rates, typically only about 20% (or less) of what your phone company would charge you. Google Voice lets you call just about anywhere in the world and has a rate already set for that location, as you can see in Figure 1.6, which displays the top of the (very long) rate sheet for Google Voice international calls.

So, yes, Google Voice does charge for international calls (not including calls to Canada), but the cost is much less than you usually pay elsewhere.

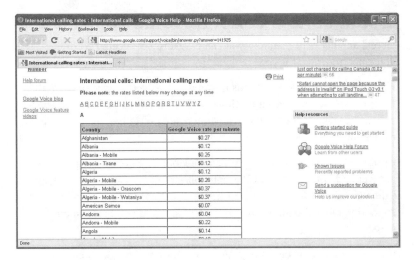

FIGURE 1.6   The International Calling Rates page.

Temporary Call Forwarding

You can also forward calls to other phones temporarily as long as you've told Google Voice about those phones on the Phones tab of the Settings page.

Temporary call forwarding is great when, for example, you're in a meeting, and you want to forward calls that would normally come to your cell to your office instead. Or you might be in a hotel and want calls to come to your room when you're out.

You can set up (and cancel) temporary call forwarding from any phone just by calling Google Voice and following the prompts—just a matter of pressing keys on a phone.

The ability to temporarily forward calls may sound exotic and like something you'd rarely use, but reasons for it come up all the time. For example, if you're called to stay with a sick relative and you want work calls to be forwarded to your mobile phone while you're there, then temporary call forwarding is your ticket.

Text Messaging

Text messaging wasn't invented by Google Voice, but Google Voice has improved it.

First, all text messages are free. While other carriers might charge hefty fees for text messages, Google Voice doesn't charge a penny for them. (Free text messaging applies in the U.S. and Canada only—you can't send text messages to other international destinations yet).

Second, Google Voice makes composing text messages much easier. Even if your mobile phone has a full keyboard, those keys are usually tiny. On other phones, sending a text message can be time-consuming and frustrating, as you press 9 four times to get a "z," then 6 three times to get an "o," or try to remember how to switch to uppercase or numbers. Now you can send text messages from your computer's full-size keyboard.

To compose a text message using the Google Voice web page, click the SMS button, and a drop-down box appears, as shown in Figure 1.7.

FIGURE 1.7 The SMS drop-down box.

PLAIN ENGLISH: **SMS**

SMS is the techie name for text messages. It stands for *Short Message Service*.

Just type in the phone number you're texting, followed by your message, and click the Send button.

SMS messages show up in your Inbox for easy tracking, and you can
search through them for text matches. You can also click the SMS link on
any Google Voice page (it's on the left) to open the SMS box in the center
pane, showing all your SMS messages. Lesson 7, "Text Messaging," tells
you more about using Google Voice to send and receive text messages.

Switching Phones During an Incoming Call

Have you ever been heading out the door, only to get a call on your landline? With Google Voice, that's not a problem—just answer the ringing
phone, press a few keys, transfer the call to your cell phone, and be on
your way. That's because Google Voice makes it easy for you to switch
phones during a call.

For example, in this scenario when you pick up a landline phone as you're
heading off for the beach, you could switch the call to your mobile phone
and continue to chat. No more being tied to a landline.

Recording Phone Calls

Being able to record calls as you talk is another handy feature of Google
Voice. When you're on a call you want to record, just click a few buttons
on your phone. This feature is useful if you want a record of a call or, say,
the boss is giving you instructions and you want to make sure you remember all the details.

Recorded calls are sent to your Inbox, and you can play them back with a
click of a button. Note that Google Voice makes no attempt to transcribe
recorded calls into text. That's because figuring out who said what
when—that is, keeping the speakers straight—is too complex.

> TIP
> In some states, it's illegal to record someone's call without their
> knowledge. Accordingly, Google Voice always announces that the call
> is being recorded to both parties—you and the person who called
> you.

Conference Calling on the Fly

How do you usually set up a conference call? First, there's the slow and arduous process of setting a time, which can involve many calls or emails. Then you have to get a conference number. Then you get an access code. Then you send out that info to everybody and hope they call in at the appointed time.

Google Voice can help you make that process easier. Instead of getting a conference phone number and sharing that with everyone, then getting an access code and sharing that with everyone, all you need to do is to tell them to call your Google Voice number.

Conference calling won't work unless you have call waiting on your phone. When people call, you can admit them to the conference call one at a time. That way, all the people you want to talk to can join the conversation. Not bad, eh?

> TIP
> At this time, you have to keep the conference fairly small—four or fewer callers.

Using Call Widgets

This feature is a little more snazzy than essential. You can use Google Voice to create call widgets that you embed in a web page, making it easy for visitors to your website to call you.

You create and keep track of call widgets on the Call Widgets tab of the Settings page, shown in Figure 1.8.

When you create a call widget, you customize it with the Google Voice number to call, and Google Voice gives you a snippet of HTML code that you can copy and embed in a web page.

A call widget embedded on a web page looks just as you see in Figure 1.8—a small icon that displays a phone and is labeled "Call Me." When visitors to your website want to contact you, they click the widget, which displays text boxes for the caller's phone number and a Call button.

FIGURE 1.8   Call widgets.

When a caller types in a phone number and clicks the Call button, Google Voice calls him back on his phone and then connects him by calling you. If you don't pick up, the call goes to voicemail.

Call widgets can be fun. If you want to drum up business by making it easy for visitors to your website to contact you, a call widget is a great idea. For most purposes, though, a call widget is a little gimmicky. After all, it's just as easy to display your phone number on your website—and just as easy for people to contact you by dialing that number, rather than using the call widget. Still, a widget can get visitors' attention.

Call widgets do offer a real advantage, however, when you don't want to make your phone number public. Posting a phone number on a web page can be an open invitation to getting on a telemarketing or other list, opening the door to all kinds of unwanted calls. So if you want people to call, but you don't want them to have your number, call widgets are a great solution. And even if you're not trying to hide your phone number, a call widget still looks cool.

Goog411

Google Voice's free directory assistance, Goog411, is a very useful feature, especially for mobile phones. Charges for directory assistance have skyrocketed, and that's especially true for mobile phones. Currently, Verizon charges $1.99 for mobile directory assistance, and landlines aren't that far behind.

Goog411 can save you a couple of bucks when you need to get a phone number. Here's how you access it:

1. Dial your Google Voice number. Google Voice picks up and asks you to state your name.

2. During the recording, press *. Google Voice responds with a beep.

3. Enter your four-digit PIN (unless you've told Google Voice not to require a PIN). Google Voice responds with a phone menu.

4. Press 3 for Goog411.

5. At the prompt, say the name of the listing you want and the city and state. Google Voice repeats your entry and connects you.

> **NOTE**
> How good is Goog411's voice recognition? Very good. On tests I've made myself, Goog411 has recognized even difficult names that completely stumped the toll-free 800-number directory assistance (800-555-1212) voice recognition system.

How Google Voice Works

It's easy to sign up for Google Voice, as you see in Lesson 2, "Signing Up and Getting Started." Just give Google some information, and you're in. (Note that at this writing, you need to have an invitation to Google Voice before you can sign up—you see how to request one in the next lesson).

You can get a new Google Voice number, or you can set up Google Voice to use the number of your mobile phone.

After signing up, you can add more phones to your account. When you tell Google Voice about other phones, you can forward calls to those phones.

The whole sign-up and sign-in process is coming up in the next lesson. But before we jump in to Lesson 2, let's take a look at a few more general points about Google Voice.

How Much Does Google Voice Cost?

Signing up for and using Google Voice is free. Sending text messages is free. Getting directory assistance is free. Let's hope all these features always stay free. You can't beat free.

Making some calls is the only thing that's not completely free. Calls to the U.S. and Canada are free, but international calls aren't. They're cheap, though, as discussed earlier (and in more detail in Lesson 9, "Billing and International Calls"). You can add money to your account using a credit card, and then you can call internationally. You start off with a credit of ten cents when you sign up, which isn't very much, so be sure to add money to your account before you make an international call.

How Good Is the Call Quality?

Google works hard to make sure that call quality is good, working continually with call carriers to monitor and correct any problems. Google also listens to your feedback to learn about any problems. In general, you should get as good of quality calls with Google Voice as you would with any standard carrier.

You can give Google feedback on call quality if you click the Placed link on the left of any Google Voice page. A record of the calls you've placed opens, as shown in Figure 1.9.

On the right in every placed call's record are two boxes—a box with a checkmark in it and a box with an X in it. Select one of those options to make your opinion known about the quality of the call.

Of course, quality becomes a bigger issue when you're actually paying for the call. When you make an international call and the call quality is poor, you can request a refund, as Lesson 9 explains.

NOTE

Google Voice only makes refunds for short international calls. Their assumption is that if you stuck with the call for several minutes, the call quality must have been OK.

FIGURE 1.9   Looking at placed calls.

What Are the System Requirements?

To use Google Voice, you'll need a touch-tone phone, as well as a computer running one of these operating systems:

- ► Windows XP

- ► Windows Vista

- ► Mac

- ► Linux

TIP

Google Voice doesn't list Windows 7 in its list of acceptable operating systems yet, but our informal tests indicate that Google Voice appears to work just fine in Windows 7.

As far as web browsers go, you'll need

- ► IE6 or above

- ► Firefox 3 or above

- ► Safari 3 or above

- ► Google Chrome

In addition, your browser needs to support Flash 8 or higher.

That's it! You've probably already got the equipment and the software you need to use Google Voice.

Summary

Now that you know what Google Voice is, how it works, and what equipment it requires, it's time to put Google Voice to work. In Lesson 2 you'll sign up for a Google Voice account and set it up to manage your phones.

LESSON 2

Signing Up and Getting Started

Lesson 1, "Welcome to Google Voice," showed you all the great reasons to use Google Voice. Now it's time to put Google Voice to work. Before you can start to explore Google Voice's features, you need to sign up and set up your phones.

Getting started with Google Voice is quick and easy:

- ▶ Request an invitation.
- ▶ Sign up for Google Voice.
- ▶ Register your phone.
- ▶ Add more phones.

Currently, you need an invitation to join Google Voice. (If that's changed by the time you read this, skip ahead to the "Setting Up Your Google Voice Account" section.) So let's start with the process of requesting an invitation.

Requesting an Invitation

Navigate your browser to www.google.com/voice, which appears in Figure 2.1.

That's the page you see when you first go to Google Voice. Note that you must sign in using a Google account using the two text boxes at the right.

Here's the catch: Even if you have a Google account, you can't actually sign in unless your account is enabled for Google Voice. As of this writing, you need an invitation to Google Voice before you can sign in. So don't try to sign in unless you've been invited to Google Voice.

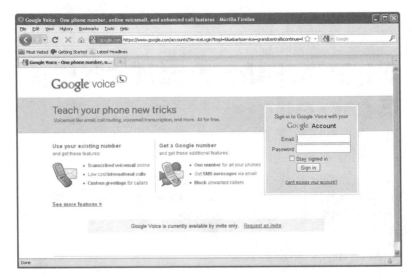

FIGURE 2.1   The Google Voice signup page.

TIP

When Google Voice goes public, you'll be able to sign in with just a Google account, no invitation necessary. How do you know if you still need an invitation when you read this? Take a look at the Google Voice page at www.google.com/voice, which appears in Figure 2.1. If you see the text "Google Voice is currently available by invite only," you still need an invitation. If you don't see that line, just enter your Google account information and click the Sign In button. Don't have an account? We'll get you one in a page or two.

So how do you request an invitation? Just follow these steps:

1. Navigate to the Google Voice website at www.google.com/voice.

2. Click the **Request an Invite** link at the bottom of the page. This opens the page you see in Figure 2.2.

3. Enter your name.

4. Enter your email address.

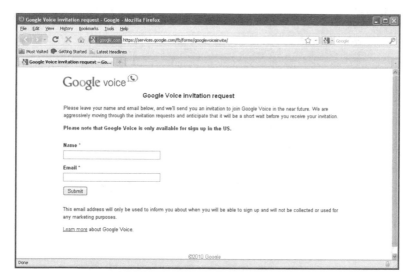

FIGURE 2.2   Requesting an invitation.

5. Click the **Submit** button. Doing so opens a page that thanks you for your interest in Google Voice and lets you know you will get an invitation when Google opens Google Voice to more users.

Now you have to wait for Google to send you an invitation. If Google Voice has a long list of potential invitees, it might take a while for you to receive your invitation, so be patient.

TIP

If you're not particularly patient, you can receive an invitation more quickly by getting a friend who already has Google Voice to invite you to try it out. See the "Inviting Others to Google Voice" section in this lesson to let your friend know how to invite you.

Congratulations! You've Been Invited!

When your invitation arrives, it will be an email from "Google Voice." The email contains a link; clicking that link opens the page you see in Figure 2.3.

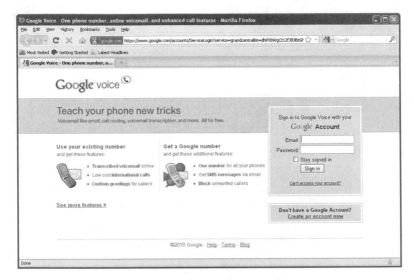

FIGURE 2.3   The post-invitation page.

This looks very much like the Google Voice page shown in Figure 2.1, but note that this page *doesn't* have the line saying, "Google Voice is currently available by invite only."

Instead, you're being asked to log in with a Google account or to create a Google account now.

If Your Invitation Link Doesn't Work

Occasionally, the invitation links sent out by Google Voice fail. If that happens to you, here are some things to consider:

- ▶ **Has your link already been used?** You can only use a Google invitation once—it can't be reused. If you or someone else has already used the invitation you received, that's it—the invitation has expired, and you'll get an "Object Not Found" error if you try to access it.

- ▶ **Is the link being launched properly?** If your email program isn't launching the link and opening your browser when you click that link, try copying the link and pasting it into your browser's address box. Sometimes that solves the problem.

▶ **Are you trying to sign in with Google Apps?** It's not possible to use Google Voice with a Google Apps account. You need to use an existing Google Account or create a new one. At some point in the future, it may be possible to sign in with a Google Apps account, but not yet.

> NOTE
> What's the difference between Google Apps and a Google Account? Google Apps is a suite of services for businesses, schools, and organizations. A Google Account, on the other hand, is for individuals and gives you access to a wide range of Google services for consumers, including Gmail, Picasa Web Albums (Google's online photo-sharing service), Google Calendar, Blogger, iGoogle, and a whole lot more. If you've ever used any of those services, you already have a Google Account—go to www.google.com/accounts and sign in with the email address you use to sign into other Google services.

If You Have a Google Account

If you already have a Google Account, which means you have an email address and password that you can use to log into a Google service such as Gmail, you're all set at this stage. Enter that information, click the Sign In button, and skip ahead to the "Setting Up Your Google Voice Account" section.

Otherwise, take a look at the next section to create a Google Account.

Create Your Google Account

You'll need a Google account to sign into Google Voice, so if you don't have one, create one now. First, click the link that appears in your invitation email from Google Voice (or, if Google Voice is no longer requiring invitations, simply go to www.google.com/voice) and follow these steps:

1. Click the **Create an Account Now** link. The page you see in Figures 2.4 and 2.5 opens.

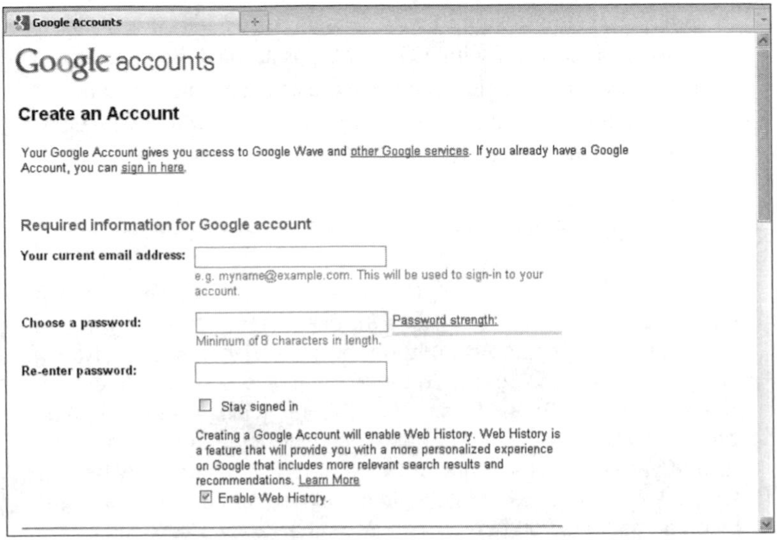

FIGURE 2.4   The Google Create an Account page, top.

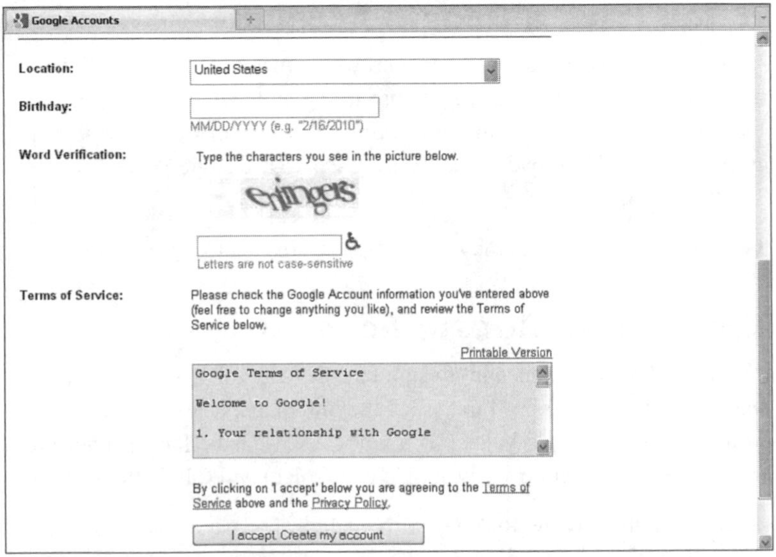

FIGURE 2.5   The Google Create an Account page, bottom.

> TIP
>
> You can also create a Google Account by going directly to
> www.google.com/accounts, clicking the **Create an Account Now**
> link, and then following steps listed here.

2. Enter your email address in the Your Current Email Address box. This is your current email address, which you will use to sign into your Google account as your username.

3. Think of a good, strong password that's hard for others to guess and enter it in the Choose a Password box. Your password should be a minimum of eight characters in length.

   As you type in your password, the page displays a horizontal bar indicating password strength—that is, how hard the password would be for someone else to guess. For maximum password strength, use a combination of letters and numbers.

4. Re-enter your password in the second password box. To make sure there are no typos in your password, Google checks that the two passwords agree.

5. Leave the Stay Signed In checkbox checked if you want to stay signed in after you've created your account. If you uncheck this box, you'll have to sign in to Google Voice each time you go to the Google Voice page.

6. Check or uncheck the **Enable Web History** checkbox. When you create a Google Account, Web History is automatically enabled. This service helps to personalize your search results. Here's how Google puts it: Web History provides you with "a more personalized experience on Google that includes more relevant search results and recommendations."

7. In the Get Started with Google Voice section, select your country in the Location box. The default is the United States.

8. Enter your birthday in MM/DD/YYYY format. So if you were born on October 22, 1983, for example, you'd type in *10/22/1983*.

9. In the Word Verification section, take a look at the characters shown in the distorted image and type those characters into the text box. In Figure 2.5, you'd type *entingers*.

> TIP
>
> Can't make out the wavy letters in the Word Verification section? Make sure your computer's speakers are on, and click the blue handicap icon. Google reads the letters to you out loud so you can type them in.

10. Read the Terms of Service in the scrollable box. If you want, you can also click the **Privacy Policy** link to open Google's privacy policy in a new window and read that, too.

11. Click the **I Accept. Create My Account** button.

Google Accounts opens a page telling you that you've successfully created your account and will send you an email to verify the email address you gave.

At this point, Google Voice reappears, as shown in Figure 2.6, asking you to configure your account. We do that next in the "Setting Up Your Google Voice Account" section.

FIGURE 2.6   Choose a Google Voice option.

12. Open the verification em
Accounts opens a page

Now that you've got a G
your Google Voice ac

Setting Up You
Account

At this point, you come to a fork in the road, as F₁ᵦ
when you create a new Google Voice account, Google a
how you're going to use Google Voice:

▶ With an existing mobile phone number

▶ With a brand new phone number that works for all of your
phones

Which one should you pick? It depends on what you want Google Voice to
do for you:

▶ **Get Google Voicemail:** The main advantage here is that you
don't have to give out a new number to family, friends, and contacts to get these Google Voice benefits (described in detail in
Lesson 1):

   ▶ Voicemail

   ▶ Transcribed voicemail sent to your email inbox

   ▶ Custom greetings

   ▶ Low-cost international calling

   ▶ Notifications

   ▶ The ability to share voicemail

NOTE

You must already have a mobile phone to choose Get Google
Voicemail.

Google Number: When you request a new number
gle (it's free) to manage all your phones, you get all
res just listed, plus a few more:

A single number that can ring any or all of your phones

▶ Free SMS text messaging

▶ Caller screening

▶ Call-blocking ability

▶ Call-screening ability

Here's what the decision boils down to:

▶ If you want to use Google Voice's basic features on your mobile
phone without having to give out a new phone number, choose
Get Google Voicemail.

▶ If you want all of Google Voice's features and a single number
to manage all of your phones, choose Get a New Google
Number.

Signing Up for a Google Voice Phone Number

If you want to manage multiple phones, each with its own number—such
as the landline in your home, a couple of mobile phones, and your work
phone—choose the option to sign up for a Google Voice phone number.
From the Google Voice signup page (www.google.com/voice/signup),
click Get a New Google Number. The page shown in Figure 2.7 opens.
From there, follow these steps:

1. Choose your new Google Voice phone number. This will be the
new number that people will call to contact you (it can ring any
or all of your phones or go straight to voicemail), so choose
well.

   You can search for available numbers by entering your current
area code or ZIP code. You can also search for an easy-to-
remember word (such as your last name), phrase, or number to

use as the basis for your new phone number. Click **Search**, and Google suggests a number, as shown in Figure 2.7. If you don't like the number, you can search again. If the number looks good, click its radio button and then click **Continue**.

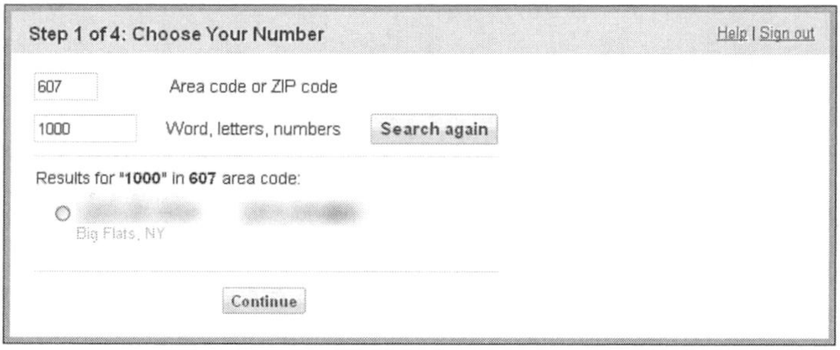

FIGURE 2.7 Search for a number.

2. Choose a PIN. To pick up voicemail messages over a phone (see Lesson 5, "Using Voicemail"), you need a four-digit access code. You select your PIN in the dialog box shown in Figure 2.8. Type the PIN you want (and then again to confirm it) and check the box to tell Google you agree with its Terms and Privacy Policy for using Google Voice. Click **Continue** to move on to Step 3.

3. Add a forwarding phone. Google Voice shows the dialog box shown in Figure 2.9. Add the phone you want to ring when someone calls your new Google Voice number. (You can add more phones later.)

Make sure it's a phone that you can answer right now because you'll have to verify the phone number in the next step. Type in the phone number and select the phone's type (home, work, and so on) from the drop-down list. Click **Continue**.

4. Verify your phone. Next, confirm the number of your forwarding phone. As Figure 2.10 shows, Google gives you a two-digit verification code. When you click the **Call Me Now** button, Google dials your forwarding phone number and, after you've answered, prompts you to enter the verification code. After you've done that, you'll have a chance to record your name and a voicemail greeting. (If you'd rather do that later, just hang up.)

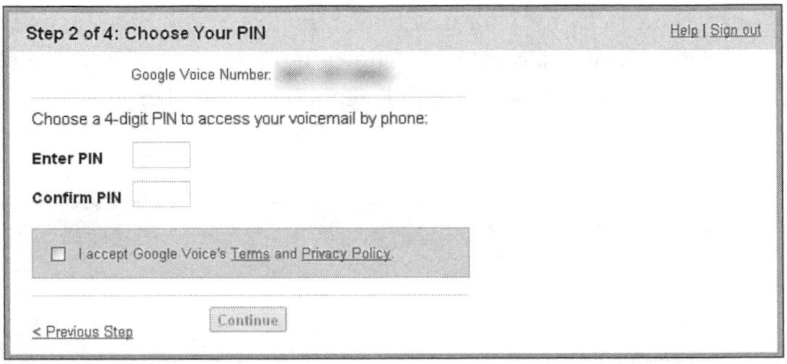

FIGURE 2.8   Choose a PIN.

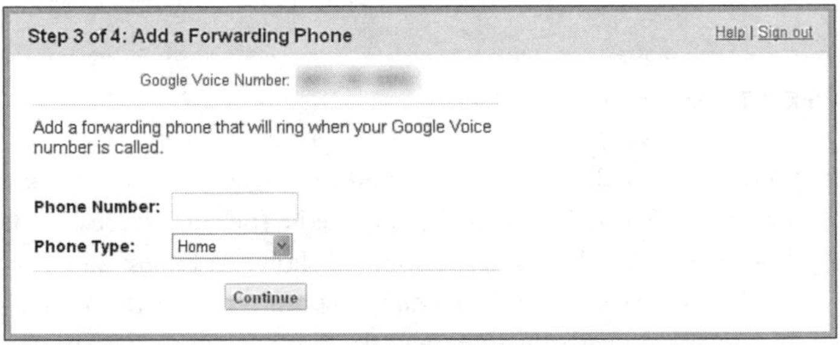

FIGURE 2.9   Add a forwarding phone.

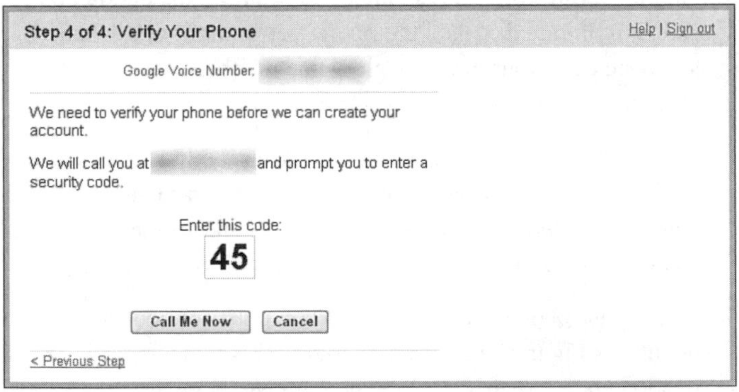

FIGURE 2.10   A verification code.

After you've completed these steps, Google congratulates you for successfully setting up your new Google Voice account, as shown in Figure 2.11. You can click the **Add More Phones** link to set up additional phones with your account (you can learn more about that later in this chapter) or click **Done!** to go to your Google Voice Inbox (flip ahead to Figure 2.14 to see it).

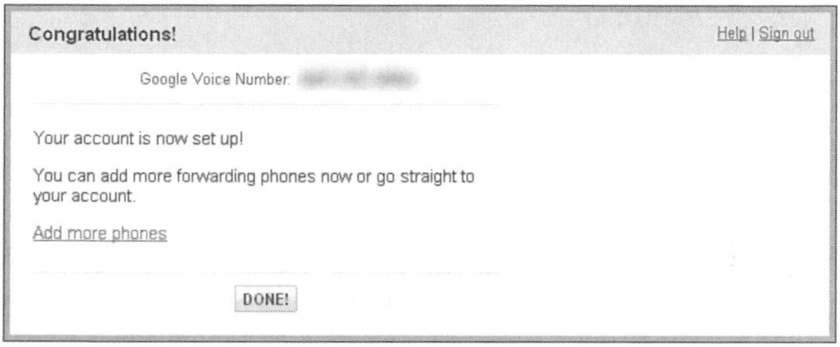

FIGURE 2.11   Welcome to Google Voice!

Signing Up for Google Voice with an Existing Mobile Phone Number

Maybe you don't want a new phone number to hand out to everyone who calls you. If you want to use Google-style voicemail for your mobile phone (and yes, it has to be a mobile phone to use this option), first make sure that your phone is turned on and close at hand. Then click the big, blue **Set Up Your Phone** button (if you no longer have the signup page in your browser, go to www.google.com/voice and log in to get to this page, which is shown to all new users), shown back in Figure 2.6. Signing up has four steps:

1. Tell Google your phone number. Enter your existing phone number (including area code) and choose your mobile carrier from the drop-down list, as shown in Figure 2.12. Then click **Continue**.

2. Verify your phone number. You'll see a dialog box like the one shown in Figure 2.10. Click **Call Me Now**, and when Google prompts you for the verification code, enter it. Record your name and a voice greeting if you want, or do that later.

FIGURE 2.12   Enter your mobile phone number and carrier.

3. Choose a PIN. After Google has verified your phone number, the dialog box on your computer screen changes to look like the one in Figure 2.8. Here, you choose a four-digit PIN that will let you get your voicemail on your phone (see Lesson 5). Type in your PIN and then type it in again to confirm it. Check the box to agree with Google's terms of service and privacy policy and then click **Continue**.

4. Set up your phone. In the last step, shown in Figure 2.13, Google displays a long string of characters. Enter these characters into your phone and then press its Call or Send button. Your phone displays a confirmation message. Your Google Voice account is all set up!

5. Click **Continue**.

Now you can start using Google Voice with your mobile phone.

After you've set up your account, Google gives you a number you can call when you want to check your voicemail. You can call this number from any phone and use your PIN to listen to voicemail messages. (Of course, you can also check your voicemail on the Google Voice website—see Lesson 5.) If you want, make a note of the number or add it to your Phonebook. If you don't do either of those, though, don't worry—the number is prominently featured at the top of all pages in your Google Voice account.

FIGURE 2.13   Set up your mobile phone.

The Google Voice Inbox

After you've set up your Google Voice account, click **Show Me My Inbox** to start using Google Voice. The Inbox appears as you see in Figure 2.14.

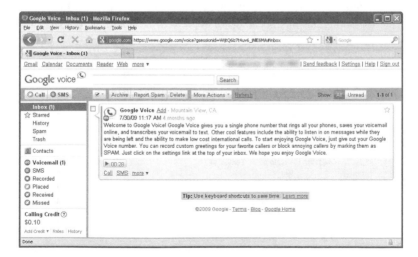

FIGURE 2.14   Your Inbox.

The Inbox is where all your voicemail transcripts and text messages will appear, as discussed in Lesson 1. You can see in Figure 2.14 that Google Voice has already sent you a welcome message giving you a brief overview of Google Voice.

And that's it—you're in. Now you've got a username (the email address you used to create your Google account) and password. Next time you want to log in, just go to www.google.com/voice and enter that email address, your password, and click the **Sign In** button. Google Voice will respond by displaying your Inbox, as shown in Figure 2.14.

Want to invite others to join Google Voice too? Take a look at the next section.

Inviting Others to Google Voice

Now that you have your own Google Voice account, it's easy to invite friends and associates to Google Voice, too. (Of course, this won't be necessary when Google Voice no longer requires invitations, although you can always use your invitations to spread the word about Google Voice.)

To send an invitation, follow these steps:

1. Navigate to the Google Voice site and sign in if necessary. The Google Voice site appears in your browser.

2. In the lower left part of the page, click the **Invite a Friend** link. Clicking this link opens the dialog box you see in Figure 2.15.

FIGURE 2.15 Inviting a friend.

3. Enter the email address of the person you want to invite.

4. Edit the invitation message if you wish.

5. Click the **Send Invites** button.

Google Voice sends an invitation to the people whose email addresses you've entered. (You can send a total of three invitations.) The recipients get invited immediately through email. All a recipient has to do is to click the link in the email and complete the signup process, described earlier in this lesson.

Adding Phones to Google Voice

When you created your Google Voice account, you told Google about your primary phone number. But Google Voice is designed to let you work with all your phones. You can also add other phones to Google Voice and work with them, as well.

To add a new phone to Google Voice, follow these steps:

1. Navigate to the Google Voice site and sign in if necessary. The Google Voice site appears in your browser.

2. Click the **Settings** link to open the Settings page.

3. Click the **Phones** tab to view the phones currently registered with your Google Voice number.

4. Click the **Add Another Phone Link**. Doing so opens the page you see in Figure 2.16.

4. Enter a name for the new phone. The new name is the English-language name for the phone, such as "My Mobile."

5. Enter the number of the phone.

6. Select the type of phone you're adding. These are your choices:

  ▶ Mobile

  ▶ Work

  ▶ Home

  ▶ Other

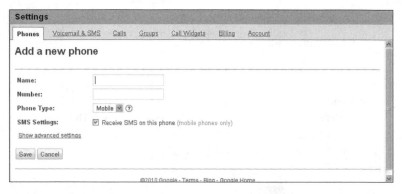

FIGURE 2.16 Adding a new phone.

7. Check the **Receive SMS on This Phone (Mobile Phones Only)** checkbox if you want to use this phone to send and receive text messages.

   The Show Advanced Settings link lets you set Voicemail access (covered in Lesson 3, "Making a Call") and set a ring schedule (covered in Lesson 4, "Answering a Call").

8. Click the **Save** button to save the new phone. Google Voice displays a dialog box that tells you it needs to confirm the new phone and displays a two-digit verification code.

9. Click the **Connect** button in the dialog box. Google Voice calls you on the new phone.

10. Pick up the phone. Google Voice asks you to enter your two-digit verification code.

11. Enter the verification code on the phone. Google Voice confirms your new phone and hangs up.

Now you've added a new phone to your Google Voice account. You can manage this phone using Google Voice, along with the phone you used to set up your account.

Removing Phones from Google Voice

After you've added one or more phones to Google Voice, those phone numbers appear on the Phones tab of the Settings page. If you decide you want to remove a phone from your Google Voice account, follow these steps:

1. Navigate to the Google Voice site and sign in if necessary. The Google Voice site appears in your browser.

2. Click the **Settings** link to open the Settings page.

3. Click the **Phones** tab to view the phones currently registered with your Google Voice number.

4. Find the number you want to delete. Click the **Delete** button below it.

5. Google asks you to confirm that you want to delete the phone. Click **OK**.

That phone number is no longer registered with Google Voice.

Converting a Google Voice Mobile Account to a Full Google Voice Account

If you signed up to use Google Voice with a single mobile phone, you might soon decide that you want the benefits of a full Google Voice account for all your phones. Here's how to convert a single-phone Google Voice mobile account to a full account:

1. Navigate to the Google Voice site and sign in if necessary. The Google Voice site appears in your browser.

2. Click the **Settings** link to open the Settings page.

3. Click the **Phones** tab to view the Google voicemail access number for your mobile phone.

4. Beside your access number, click the **Get a Google Number** link.

5. The Upgrade to a Google Number dialog box opens, listing some of the benefits of a full Google Voice account. Click **Continue**.

6. Search for a number by entering your ZIP Code and/or a word or phrase on which to base your Google Voice number. Click **Search**.

7. Google Voice shows you a list of possible numbers. If you don't like any of the possibilities, you can click **Search Again** or **Next 5** to see more numbers. When you see a number you want, choose it by activating its radio button, and click **Continue**.

8. Google Voice confirms this as your new Google Voice number. Click **Continue**.

9. Google Voice sends you a confirmation code. Use your mobile phone's keypad to enter the number (as though you were calling someone), then press your phone's **Call** or **Send** button.

When Google Voice receives your confirmation, you've now got all the benefits of a full Google Voice account, with your mobile phone already registered.

Using Keyboard Shortcuts

Google Voice supports a number of keyboard shortcuts that can make your life easier. For reference, you'll find the Google Voice single-key shortcuts in Table 1.1 and the combination keyboard shortcuts in Table 1.2.

TABLE 1.1   Shortcut Keys

Shortcut Key	Action
c	Open Quick Call.
m	Open Quick SMS.
<Esc>	Close Quick Call or Quick SMS.
/	Jump to search box.
Right arrow or n	Go to next page.
Left arrow or p	Go to previous page.
#	Move message(s) to trash.
!	Mark message(s) as spam.
<Shift> + i	Mark as read.
<Shift> + u	Mark as unread.

TABLE 1.2   Shortcut Key Combinations

Key Combination	Action
g then i	Go to Inbox.
g then s	Go to Starred.
g then h	Go to History.
g then p	Go to Placed calls.
g then r	Go to Received calls.
g then m	Go to Missed calls.
g then c	Go to Contacts.
g then u	Go to unread messages.
* then a	Select all.
* then n	Select none.
* then r	Select read.
* then u	Select unread.

Summary

You've created a Google Voice account and set it up with some phones. But setting up your Google Voice account is just the first step. Now it's time to use it. So turn to Lesson 3 to learn about making calls.

LESSON 3

Making a Call

Lesson 2, "Signing Up and Getting Started," showed you all the basics of getting Google Voice up and running. In this chapter, we start putting Google Voice to work for us by making calls.

Many people use Google Voice purely to receive calls, taking advantage of the great features available: call filtering, call blocking, call forwarding, call recording, and so on. But Google Voice wouldn't be complete without letting you make outgoing calls.

There are many good reasons to make calls through Google Voice. One is convenience—you can use the contacts you've recorded in your Contacts (much like a phone book) and call them with ease. Calls through Google Voice are also typically cheaper than landlines or mobile phones. They're free nationally and very inexpensive internationally, so over time you can save a lot of money making calls through Google Voice.

There's another reason for using Google Voice that you might not expect: getting others to use your Google-assigned number. When you call someone, especially on a mobile phone, the recipient tends to call you back using the phone number from which you called that person. If you want your call to be returned to your Google number (so you can take advantage of all Google Voice's features), you should call people using Google Voice so your Google number displays as your callback number.

In other words, calling people from your Google Voice number means that they'll return your call to the same number. Otherwise, you'll call them on one number and ask them to call you back on a different number, which can lead to mixed results depending on your friends and contacts. So although you don't have to use Google Voice to make calls, doing so will encourage your contacts to use your Google Voice number, leading to better results.

TIP

If you're concerned about making sure you call people and receive their calls through the same number, but you don't want to make calls exclusively through Google Voice (which takes an extra step or two), you have other options. You can preserve your old number and set it up so that all incoming calls are forwarded to Google Voice. That way, you call out on your old line, and people call in on your old line, but you still use Google Voice to filter, record, and otherwise handle the calls.

You can also use your mobile number as your Google number instead of using a Google-assigned number, so when you make calls, you'll be using your mobile phone as usual, and people will call your mobile number as well—problem solved.

In fact, there are some SmartPhones that you can program so that you simply enter the number to call, and the SmartPhone will call your Google Voice number and make the call for you through Google Voice. Perhaps in the future we'll see this functionality on more mobile phones.

Making Google Voice Calls

There are two ways to place calls through Google Voice: computer-assisted and through your Google-assigned number.

When you make a computer-assisted call, you tell Google Voice not only what number you want to call, but also what number you want to call from. Google Voice then calls you *and* the number you want to call and connects the two calls.

When you make a call through your Google-assigned number, you call your own Google number, press * during the message, enter your PIN, then, at the prompt, enter the number you want to call. Google Voice connects you at once.

Note that when you call out using Google Voice, you simply tell it the number to call using the area code (which you need even for local calls) and the number—don't tell it to dial a 1 first.

To make an international call, enter 011, the country code, and then the number, for example, 011442012345612345. When storing an international number in your Contacts, use a +, the country code, and then the number, such as +33 123456789.

In this lesson, we see all the ways to make calls using Google Voice, and also how to make your life a bit easier by setting up and maintaining a list of Contacts for frequently called numbers.

There are several different ways you can make a call using Google Voice:

▶ Call your own Google number, press *, key in your PIN, then follow the prompts, selecting option 2 to place a call.

▶ Click the **Call** button at the top left of the site, type a contact's name or phone number, select the phone you want to use for that call, and click the **Connect** button.

▶ In a message in your Inbox, click **Call** at the bottom of the message.

> NOTE
>
> When you enter a number into the Google Voice website and tell Google Voice to call that number for you, Google calls that method Click2Call, and it's a term you'll often see on the Google Voice site.

▶ Click any highlighted phone number in a voicemail transcript.

▶ Access the Google Voice mobile site (www.google.com/voice/m) from your mobile phone and use the Quick Call field at the bottom of the page to enter any phone number.

▶ In the Contacts Manager, click the call link beside a number.

As you can see, you either dial Google Voice or use your computer (or mobile phone's web browser) to enter a number to call.

Let's get started now by making Google Voice calls from your phone.

Using Your Phone to Make Google Voice Calls

If you're not near a computer and don't have a mobile phone with a Web browser, you can still make a Google Voice call from any phone.

The process is easy, and just involves calling your own Google-assigned number. Here's how it works by default from any touch-tone phone (we'll see how to make the process shorter in a moment):

1. Dial your Google Voice number from any phone.

2. Press * during the recorded greeting. The system prompts you to enter your PIN—not with a voice prompt, but with a simple beep.

3. Enter your PIN. Google Voice then gives you a list of options.

4. Select option 2 by pressing **2**. When you press 2, you're prompted to enter the number you want to call.

5. Enter the number you want to call, starting with the area code (do not dial a 1 first) and then the number. For international calls, enter 011, the country code, then the number.

6. Press #, which tells Google Voice that you have finished entering the number. Google Voice then connects you.

The preceding steps can be shortened by telling Google Voice to go directly to voicemail when you call your own Google Number. When you do this, you don't have to press * to get to voicemail (although you can optionally configure voicemail to still require a PIN).

By default, phones you've marked as Mobile will go directly to voicemail. But also by default, phones you marked as Work, Home, or Other will *not* go directly to voicemail and will require you to enter a PIN. (You assign phones to these categories when you add them to Google Voice, as Lesson Lesson 1, "Welcome to Google Voice," explains.) You can, however, change the settings for phones you've told Google Voice about and have marked as Work, Home, or Other. Here's how to make those phones go directly to voicemail when you call your Google Voice number, saving you some steps when you make a call:

1. Navigate to the Google Voice site and click **Settings** at the top of the page. This opens the Settings page.

2. Click the **Phones tab**. This opens the Phones tab, showing you the phones you've registered with Google Voice.

3. Click the **Edit** button under the phone whose voicemail settings you want to change.

4. Click the **Show Advanced Settings** link. This opens the Advanced Settings page for the phone you've selected.

5. In the Voicemail Access section

   ▶ Select **Yes** to have direct access to voicemail. Then select the **PIN Required** or the **PIN Not Required** radio button to specify whether or not you need to enter your PIN.

   ▶ Select **No** to stop direct access to your voicemail, which means you need to press * and enter your PIN to check voicemails from this phone.

6. Click the **Save** button to save your new setting.

On a phone that's been configured to go directly to voicemail, making a call using Google Voice is a snap—just follow these quick steps:

1. Dial your Google Voice number. Pick up any phone and dial your Google Voice number.

2. Select option 2 by pressing **2**. When you press 2, you'll be prompted to enter the number you want to call.

3. Enter the number you want to call, starting with the area code (do not dial a 1 first) and then the number. For international calls, enter 011, the country code, then the number.

4. Press #. Pressing # tells Google Voice that you've finished entering the number. Google Voice then connects you.

That's how to make a call by calling in to Google Voice—every other way to make a call requires you to use a Google Voice site and have Google Voice call both you and the number you intend to call (Click2Call).

Using the Call Button

Point your browser to the Google Voice site, www.google.com/voice, and sign in. A Call button appears at the upper left part of the screen, just below the Google Voice logo, as shown in Figure 3.1.

Call button

FIGURE 3.1   Use the Call button to make a call.

To make a call through Google Voice, follow these steps:

1. Navigate to the Google Voice site.

2. Click the **Call** button. Clicking the Call button opens a drop-down window, as shown in Figure 3.2.

FIGURE 3.2   The Call button's drop-down window.

3. Enter the number you want to call in the **Call** box, starting with the area code (do not enter a 1 first) and then the number. For

international calls, enter 011, the country code, and then the number.

4. Google Voice lists the phones you've connected to Google Voice. Select the phone you want to use to make the call.

> **TIP**
>
> If you want Google Voice to always call you on the phone you've just selected (unless you make a different selection later on), select the Remember My Choice check box.

5. Click **Connect**. Google Voice calls you first on the phone you've selected. When you pick up that phone, you'll hear the other phone ringing. When the person you're calling answers, the call is completed.

6. To close the drop-down window that appeared when you clicked the Call button, click the **X** button at the upper right in the drop-down window.

Congratulations—you've just made your first Click2Call phone call!

Returning a Call

You can also call people via messages in your Inbox—just click the **Call** link at the bottom of the message.

By default, when someone calls your Google Voice number and leaves a voicemail, Google Voice transcribes that voicemail and sends it to your Inbox. (Transcribed voicemail is the main reason many people use Google Voice.) In the message, a Call link appears at the bottom. Click the link to call the person who left the message.

You can see what this Call link looks like in the message that appears in the Inbox in Figure 3.3.

Here's how to call someone back via a message that person left you:

1. Navigate to the Google Voice site and open your Inbox. You open the Inbox by clicking the **Inbox** link at left.

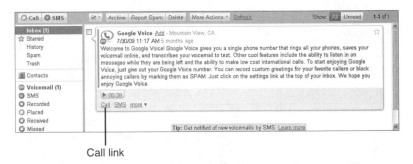

Call link

FIGURE 3.3   The Call link at the bottom of a message.

2. Click the **Call** link at the bottom of the message from the person you'd like to call back. Google Voice opens a drop-down window as shown in Figure 3.4.

FIGURE 3.4   The Call link's drop-down window.

3. Google Voice lists the phones you've connected to Google Voice. Select the phone you want to use to make the call. (If you always want Google Voice to make a call using this phone, check the **Remember My Choice** check box. You can always change your choice later.)

4. Click **Connect**. Google Voice calls you first on the phone you've selected. When you pick up that phone, you'll hear the other phone ringing. When the person you're calling answers, the call is completed.

5. To close the drop-down window that appeared when you clicked the Call button, click the **X** button at upper right.

This technique is a handy way to call someone back—no matter when that person called you.

Clicking a Highlighted Number in a Message

Here's a cool feature. When a caller leaves messages for you, that person might also tell you what number to use to call back. For example, a colleague might say, "I'll be at the Phoenix office until 4:00 today. Call me there at 602-555-6767." When Google Voice transcribes the message, it makes the phone number into a link. You can return the call simply by clicking that link.

You can see a highlighted number in the message shown in Figure 3.5.

FIGURE 3.5 Click a highlighted number to call it back.

When you click a highlighted phone number in a message, the Call button's drop-down window opens, so it's just like you'd clicked the Call button with the added convenience that Google Voice automatically puts the number you're calling into the Call box.

To call a highlighted number in a message, follow these steps:

1. Navigate to the Google Voice site and open your Inbox.

2. Click the highlighted number you want to call inside the message that contains it. Google Voice opens the Call button's drop-down window. The number to call will already be filled in.

3. Google Voice lists the phones you've connected to Google Voice. Select the phone you want to use to make the call. (If you always want Google Voice to make a call using this phone,

check the **Remember My Choice** check box. You can always change your choice later.)

4. Click **Connect**. Google Voice calls you first on the phone you've selected. When you pick up that phone, you'll hear the other phone ringing. When the person you're calling answers, the call is completed.

5. To close the drop-down window that appeared when you clicked the Call button, click the **X** button.

Using Google's Mobile Page

Google Voice has a site designed for mobile phone users—all you need is a browser in your cell phone to access it. The site is www.google.com/m, and you can place calls from there.

To place a call from the mobile site, just follow these steps:

1. Navigate to the Google Voice mobile site. The Google Voice mobile site appears in your mobile phone's browser. The site will look something like what's shown in Figure 3.6.

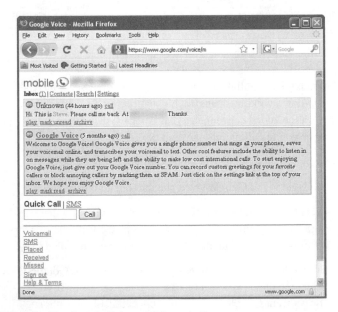

FIGURE 3.6 The Google Voice mobile website.

2. Click the **Call** button to open a drop-down window, as shown in Figure 3.6.

3. Enter the number you want to call in the Quick Call box, starting with the area code (do not dial a 1 first) and then the number. For international calls, enter 011, the country code, and then the number.

4. Click the **Call** button. Clicking the Call button opens the Google Voice Call page.

5. Google Voice lists the phones you've connected to Google Voice. Select the phone you want to use to make the call.

   Google Voice remembers the phone you choose. The next time you make a call from the Google Voice mobile page, Google Voice automatically selects that phone.

6. Click **Call**. Google Voice calls you first on the phone you've selected. When you pick up that phone, you'll hear the other phone ringing. When the person you're calling answers, the call is completed.

When you've ended the call, your mobile phone still shows the Google Voice mobile Call page, so it's up to you to navigate away from that page when you're done making calls.

Calling a Contact

In these connected times, you can't possibly remember all the phone numbers you might want to call. Good thing you don't have to. Google Voice keeps track of your contacts, so you can call them whenever you need to get in touch. In Google, a contact includes all kinds of info about a person: name, email, address, and, of course, phone number.

You can call a contact simply by clicking the Call link in that person's page in the Contact Manager. We see how to call an existing contact in this section. How you can create and manage contacts of your own is covered later in this lesson.

To call a contact, follow these steps:

1. Navigate to the Google Voice site.

2. Click the **Contacts** link on the left. Clicking the Contacts link opens the Contacts Manager, as shown in Figure 3.7.

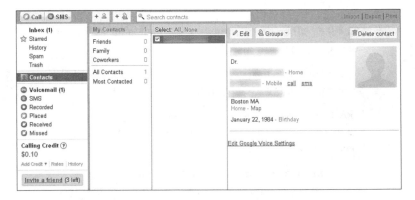

FIGURE 3.7   The Google Voice Contacts Manager.

3. Select the contact you want to call. Click the name of the contact in the Contact Manager's center column to bring up that contact's record.

4. Click the call link in the record of the contact you want to call. This opens the dialog box you see in Figure 3.8.

FIGURE 3.8   The Google Voice contact call dialog.

5. Google Voice lists the phones you've connected to Google Voice. Select the phone you want to use to make the call.

6. Click **Connect**. Google Voice calls you first on the phone you've selected. When you pick up that phone, you hear the other phone ringing. When the person you're calling answers, the call is completed.

7. To close the drop-down window that appeared when you clicked the Call button, click the **X** button.

Working with Contacts

In Google Voice, you can collect your contacts using the Contact Manager. As we've just seen, the Contact Manager makes it easy to call a contact. The rest of this lesson is all about how to create and manage your contacts.

Contacts Manager is more than just a phone book. It's an organizer that saves you time by having a central place to keep and organize information about the people you're in touch with. With just a click, you can call or email anyone whose contact information you store. (To email a contact, click the email address in that person's contact page.)

> TIP
>
> If you use Gmail or Google Talk, you'll see all your existing Gmail contacts on the Google Voice site already. Any changes to your Google Voice contacts will also be made in your other Google pages as well.

Creating a Contact

Creating a contact is easy. Just follow these steps:

1. Navigate to the Google Voice site.

2. Click the **Contacts** link on the left. Clicking the Contacts link opens the Contacts Manager, as shown in Figure 3.9. If you don't have any contacts yet, the Contacts Manager indicates that, as shown in Figure 3.9.

FIGURE 3.9   The Contacts Manager.

3. Click the **New Contact** button (that's the button with a + sign and a single person icon near the center of the page). Google Voice creates a new contact and opens it for editing, as you see in Figure 3.10.

> **NOTE**
> All fields are optional except for the contact's name.

FIGURE 3.10   Creating a new contact.

4. Enter the new contact's name. If you want, you can add information about the contact's title and company.

5. Enter the new contact's email address and select Home (the default), Work, or Other from the drop-down box. You can record as many emails for a contact as you like—just click the **add** link or the **Add** button at the bottom of the page.

6. Enter the new contact's phone number and select one of these choices from the adjacent drop-down list box:

   ▶ Home

   ▶ Work

   ▶ Mobile

   ▶ Home Fax

   ▶ Work Fax

   ▶ Pager

   ▶ Other

   You can record as many phone numbers for a contact as you like—just click the **add** link or the **Add** button at the bottom of the page.

7. Enter the new contact's address and select Home, Work, or Other from the adjacent drop-down list box.

   You can add as many addresses for a contact as you like—just click the **add** link or the **Add** button at the bottom of the page.

8. Enter the URL of the new contact's website and select one of these from the drop-down list box:

   ▶ Home

   ▶ Work

   ▶ Home Page

   ▶ FTP

   ▶ Blog

   ▶ Profile

   ▶ Other

You can list as many web sites as you like for each contact—just click the **add** link or the **Add** button at the bottom of the page.

9. Enter the new contact's birthday. Select the month, day, and year from the drop-down select boxes.

10. Enter any notes you have for the new contact in the Notes box. Notes are for whatever information you might want to remember about this contact. For example, you might note the name of a colleague's spouse here or jot down some information about a project you worked on together.

11. Click **Save** to save the new contact's information. The new contact gets added to the column at the center of the Contact Manager.

Emailing a Contact

Emailing a contact is simple. Just follow these steps:

1. Navigate to the Google Voice site.

2. Click the **Contacts** link on the left. Clicking the Contacts link opens the Contacts Manager.

3. Select the contact you want to email. Click the name of the contact in the Contact Manager's center column to bring up that contact's record.

4. Click the email address link you want to email. This opens your email program automatically. If the email address you used to sign in to Google Voice was a Gmail account, Google Voice opens a Gmail page for you, as shown in Figure 3.11.

5. Type your email and send it.

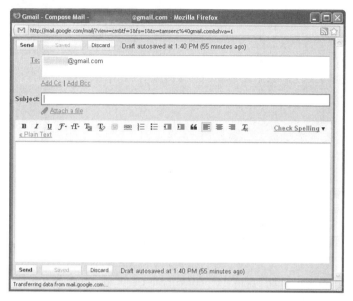

FIGURE 3.11   Emailing a contact.

Uploading a Contact's Photo

Each contact in Google Voice has a related image. When you create a
record for a new contact, the image of the contact is nothing more than a
gray, anonymous, human figure icon, which is not very helpful if you're
trying to match names with faces. To remember who's who among your
contacts, you can upload a photo of each contact, replacing that boring
icon. Just follow these steps:

1. Navigate to the Google Voice site.

2. Click the Contacts link on the left, which opens the Contacts
    Manager.

3. Click the name of the contact in the Contact Manager's center
    column to bring up that contact's record.

4. Click the anonymous human figure icon to open the Upload dia-
    log box, as shown in Figure 3.12.

FIGURE 3.12   Uploading a contact's photo.

5. Click the **Browse** button. A browser dialog box opens that lets
   you select and upload a photo from your computer. Find the
   photo you want, select it, and click the **Open** button.

   Google Voice opens the photo in the Crop this Photo dialog box,
   shown in Figure 3.13.

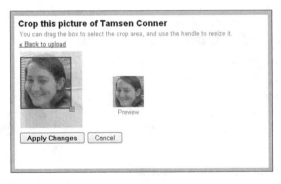

FIGURE 3.13   Cropping a contact's photo.

6. Crop the photo. Sizing handles appear on the image; click and
   drag these to crop the photo the way you want it. Click the
   Apply Changes button.

   The Suggest this Picture dialog box opens.

7. Suggest the photo to your contact—or not. If you've got a great
   photo of the contact and want to share it, you can send your

cropped photo to that person. Click the **Yes, Suggest This Picture** button to email the cropped photo to your contact with a suggestion that they use the photo themselves. Otherwise, click the **No, Keep This Picture to Myself** button to keep the photo for your own private use.

When you've completed these steps, the photo appears in the person's contact record, as shown in Figure 3.14.

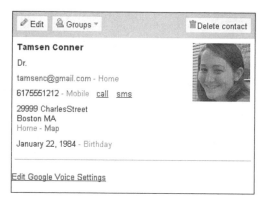

FIGURE 3.14   A contact's photo.

Deleting a Contact

Projects end. Contacts move on. When you want to delete a contact, simply do this:

1. Navigate to the Google Voice site.

2. Click the **Contacts** link on the left to open the Contacts Manager.

3. Select the contact whose record that you wish to delete.

4. Click the **Delete Contact** button. A dialog box opens, and Google Voice asks you to confirm that you want to delete the contact. Click **OK** to delete the contact's record. If you change your mind, click **Cancel** to keep the record.

Summary

You've learned the different ways you can make phone calls using Google Voice. You've also learned how to add and manage contacts to make calling even easier. Lesson 4, "Answering a Call," is all about receiving calls—how to screen your calls, work with voicemail, record calls while they're happening, forward calls to another phone, and avoid unwanted callers. So before your phone starts ringing, turn the page to read about your many options for working with incoming calls in Google Voice.

LESSON 4

Answering a Call

Lesson 3, "Making a Call," walked you through the different ways you can make a call with Google Voice. Now we discuss what Google Voice excels at—receiving calls and helping you manage them.

Receiving Calls

Google Voice is an expert at making phones ring. When you get a Google Voice number or assign your cell phone to a Google Voice number, you route incoming calls to up to six phones. So if you're on the road, for example, you can send all calls straight to your mobile phone and stop your home and work phones from ringing (your colleagues will thank you for it).

Whenever you want, you can tell Google Voice which phones to ring when there's an incoming call. To select which phones will ring when you get a call, follow these steps:

1. Navigate to the Google Voice site.

2. Click the **Settings** link, which opens the Settings page.

3. Click the **Phones** tab to open the tab, as shown in Figure 4.1.

   On the Phones tab, you see your Google Voice number displayed. Below it, the phones you've told Google Voice about appear.

4. Place a check mark next to the phones you want to have ring when your Google Voice number is called.

5. Click the **Inbox** link at left to go back to the Google Voice home page.

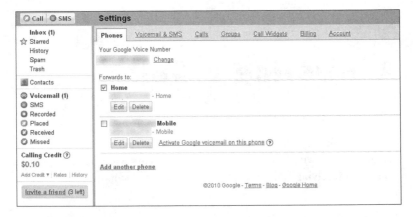

FIGURE 4.1   The Phones tab of the Settings page.

If you want, you can also add new phones to the list of incoming Google Voice calls should ring. Just follow these steps:

1. Navigate to the Google Voice site.

2. Click the **Settings** link, which opens the Settings page.

3. Click the **Phones** tab to view the phones currently connected to your Google Voice number.

4. Click the **Add Another Phone** link. This opens the page you see in Figure 4.2.

FIGURE 4.2   Adding a new phone.

4. Enter a name for the new phone. Give the phone a name that will easily identify it to you, such as "My Mobile."

5. Enter the phone number for that phone.

6. Select the type of phone you're adding. Here are your choices:

  ▶ Mobile

  ▶ Work

  ▶ Home

  ▶ Other

7. Check the **Receive SMS on This Phone (Mobile Phones Only)** checkbox if you wish to use SMS text messaging with this phone.

NOTE

The **Show Advanced Settings** link lets you set Voicemail access (covered in Lesson 3) and set a ring schedule (covered later in this lesson in "Avoiding Unwanted Calls").

---

8. Click the **Save** button to save the new phone. Google Voice shows a dialog box (shown in Figure 4.3) that tells you it needs to confirm the new phone and displays a verification code.

FIGURE 4.3   The phone verification code.

9. Click the **Connect** button in the dialog box. Google Voice calls you on the new phone.

10. Answer the phone.

11. When prompted by Google Voice, enter the verification code on the phone. Google Voice confirms your new phone and hangs up.

> TIP
>
> When you add a new mobile phone, Google Voice automatically connects you directly to voicemail when you call your Google Voice number on that phone. If that's not what you want, go to the Phones tab and click the **Edit** button under the mobile phone's entry; click the **Show Advanced Options** link and select the **No (Requires Pressing Star During Greetings—Default for Non-mobile Phones)** radio button.

You've now added the new phone to the list of available phones to which you can have calls forwarded.

> TIP
>
> Google Voice offers advanced forwarding options, too—you can forward selected calls to selected numbers, for example, or set up temporary forwarding. Read more about forwarding calls in the "Forwarding Calls" section later in this lesson.

Now when Google Voice receives an incoming call for you, it calls the phones you've selected.

What happens next? The phone rings—and then what?

What happens next is that Google Voice gives you a *Call Presentation* to announce the new call, which we explore in the following section.

Finding Out Who's Calling with Call Presentation

When someone calls your Google Voice number or a mobile phone you've connected to Google Voice, that person hears a prompt requesting his or her name. When the caller responds, Google Voice is ready to hand the call over to you.

PLAIN ENGLISH   **Call Presentation**

When someone calls your Google Voice number, you hear some audio prompts when you answer. The prompts give you several options: Send the call straight to voicemail, listen to any voicemail message as the caller leaves it, answer the call, or answer the call and start recording it. Google calls this set of choices for handling incoming calls Call Presentation.

Google Voice calls all the phones for which you've set call forwarding (see the previous section). If you answer any of those phones, Google Voice tells you that you have "a call from" and then it plays back the user's recorded name.

Google Voice then gives you two options:

▶ Press **1** to accept the call.

▶ Press **2** to send the call to voicemail.

Although you're prompted to press 1 or 2, there are actually four options available to you when you answer a call. These appear in Table 4.1.

TABLE 4.1   Options When Receiving a Call

Key	Action
1	Accept the call.
2	Send to voicemail and use ListenIn™ to listen in on the voicemail as it's being recorded.
2 then *	Join the call that's being recorded.
1 then 4	Accept and record the call.

Some people find Call Presentation annoying and simply want to receive their calls without screening them to find out who's calling. If that sounds like you, then you can turn Call Presentation off by following these steps:

1. Navigate to the Google Voice site.

2. Click the **Settings** link, which opens the Settings page.

3. Click the **Calls** tab. The Calls tab opens, as shown in Figure 4.4.

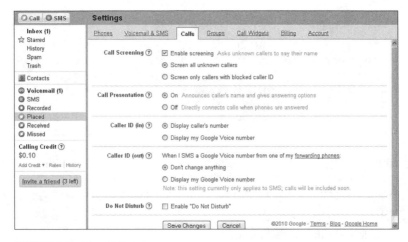

FIGURE 4.4   The Calls tab.

4. Click the **Off** radio button in the Call Presentation section to
   turn off Call Presentation.

5. Click the **Save Changes** button.

You can also turn off call screening if you don't want callers to have to
announce their names every time they call you. When you turn off call
screening, calls are simply passed through to you—and callers don't know
that they're dealing with Google Voice. To turn off call screening, and
thereby stop Google Voice from asking for each caller's name, follow
these steps:

1. Navigate to the Google Voice site.

2. Click the **Settings** link.

3. Click the **Calls** tab on the Settings page.

4. Deselect the **Enable Screening** check box to turn off call
   screening.

   Note that if you leave call screening on, you can select one of
   two options by clicking the matching radio buttons: **Screen All
   Unknown Callers** or **Screen Only Callers with Blocked
   Caller ID**.

5. Click the **Save Changes** button.

Displaying Caller ID

What about caller ID? Can you see the phone number of people who are calling you?

Yes—Google Voice passes the caller's ID on to you by default. If you have several Google Voice numbers, you can also configure Google Voice to display which Google Voice number the caller dialed. Here's how to select between these two options:

1. Navigate to the Google Voice site.

2. Click the **Settings** link.

3. Click the **Calls** tab on the Settings page.

4. Select the option you want in the **Caller ID (in)** section. The options are

   ▶ Display caller's number

   ▶ Display my Google Voice number

5. Click the **Save Changes** button. Your selection is saved.

Switching Phones During a Call

If you've ever had to put down one phone and pick up another in the middle of a call, you'll be glad to know that Google Voice allows you to switch phones without ending a call. That's useful if you need to leave the house for an appointment, for example, and you want to continue the call on your mobile phone.

If you're in the middle of a received call and you want to switch phones, press the * key.

When you do, the other phones you've connected to your Google Voice number ring. Answer any of them and keep going with your conversation. It's that simple—there are no prompts or PINs to enter, and the caller won't know anything about it.

> CAUTION
>
> You can switch phones only when you're talking on a call that you've *received* through Google Voice—not during calls that you've *placed* through Google Voice.

Screening Your Calls with ListenIn

As mentioned earlier, Google Voice lets you listen in while people are recording voicemails for you. This capability is called ListenIn, and we see how to use it here.

ListenIn is a cinch to use. When you answer a call through Google Voice, Call Presentation tells you who's calling and gives you a choice of whether to answer the call by pressing 1 or send the call to voicemail by pressing 2. If you don't hang up when you send the call to voicemail, you can hear the caller's voicemail message as it's being recorded.

Can you pick up the call if the voicemail sounds interesting enough? Yup— just press the * key. Doing so connects you to the caller immediately.

In this way, you can screen your calls with Call Presentation, listening in as the caller records a voicemail so you can decide whether this is a call you need to answer now or whether it can wait until later.

Voicemails aren't the only thing you can record. Google Voice will also record calls as they happen, as described in the next section.

Recording a Call

Google Voice has a handy feature that lets you record your incoming calls (but not the calls you make through Google Voice).

Here's how it works: When a caller dials your Google Voice number (or a mobile number you've assigned to Google Voice), it asks for the caller's name by default, so you can screen incoming calls.

Google Voice then calls you and announces the caller by playing back his or her voice. You can accept the call, record it, and save it by following these steps:

1. Press **1**. This accepts the call.

2. Press **4** at any time to start recording. Google Voice announces to both parties, "Recording on." To turn recording off during the call, press **4** again.

3. Complete the call and hang up.

4. Navigate to the Google Voice site.

5. Click the **Inbox** link. Your Inbox contains a new message corresponding to the recorded call, as you can see at the top center of Figure 4.5.

Recording box

FIGURE 4.5   Retrieving a recording.

6. Click the recording box (refer to Figure 4.5) to hear your recorded call. The call plays in its entirety (starting when the Google Voice voice says, "Recording on").

If you want to delete the recording, just delete the message. To do that, check the message's check box to the left of the message and click the **Delete** button.

Note that at this time, you can only record calls you *receive* through Google Voice. You can't record outgoing calls, including Click2Call or calls made by returning a call.

> NOTE
>
> Different areas have different laws about recording calls, so Google Voice helpfully informs you that you should check local and federal laws before you record a call. Most of these laws restrict recording a call unless both parties know about it, which is why Google Voice announces to both parties that the call is being recorded (Google Voice also announces that recording has stopped if you stop it).

Forwarding Calls

For many people, the whole attraction of Google Voice is the flexibility of its call forwarding. Google Voice offers many call forwarding options that you can configure in different ways. We looked at basic call forwarding earlier in this chapter—when you set up your Google Voice account, you indicated which phones ring when someone dials your Google Voice number. You can make up to six phones ring when you get a call by adding those phones to the Settings page's Phone tab (Figure 4.6).

FIGURE 4.6   Setting up call forwarding.

There's a lot more to call forwarding than just sending a call to up to six phones. You can forward specific callers to specific phones (this is called *conditional forwarding*). And you can turn temporary call forwarding on or off as well.

Conditional Forwarding

Conditional forwarding lets you forward specific callers to the phones you designate. So, for example, work calls could be forwarded to a particular phone and personal calls to another.

Conditional forwarding is easy in Google Voice—but before you can start playing traffic cop with incoming calls, you need to set up the appropriate callers as contacts (Lesson 3 tells you how to do that). After you've set up a particular caller as a contact, it's easy to tell Google Voice where to forward that person's calls. Just follow these steps:

1. Navigate to the Google Voice site.

2. Click the **Contacts** link to open the Contacts Manager.

3. Click the contact's name for which you want to set up forwarding. The contact's record opens, as shown in Figure 4.7.

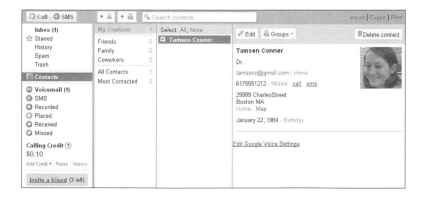

FIGURE 4.7   A contact's record.

4. Click the **Edit Google Voice Settings** link. This opens the page you see in Figure 4.8.

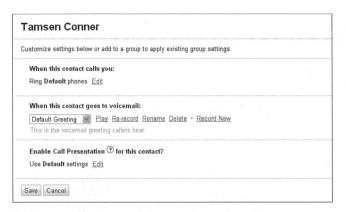

FIGURE 4.8   Editing a contact's settings.

5. Click the **Edit** link next to the Ring Default phones label. This lets you specify which phones you want to ring when the contact calls, as shown in Figure 4.9.

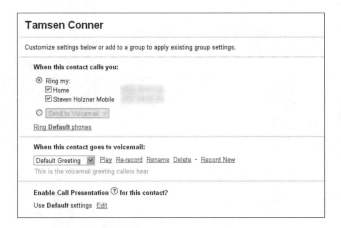

FIGURE 4.9   Specifying which phones to ring.

6. Select the phones you want to ring when this contact calls. To send the contact's calls directly to voicemail, select the **Send to Voicemail** radio button.

7. Click the **Save** button. Google Voice saves your changes.

Using Temporary Call Forwarding

Temporary call forwarding is useful when you'll be at a different phone for a limited time. Say, for example, that you're on the road and you want your Google Voice calls forwarded to your hotel phone. You can set up temporary call forwarding, which temporarily adds a new number to ring, in addition to your other phones.

Here's how to set up temporary call forwarding:

1. Call your Google number.

2. Press * and then enter your PIN if you're calling from a phone you haven't set up for forwarding with Google Voice, or just enter your PIN if you're calling from a phone that you've already set up for forwarding.

3. Press **4**. This lets you access the main settings menu.

4. Press **4** again. This lets you access your temporary settings.

5. Press **2**. This lets you set up a temporary forwarding number.

6. Press # to add the number you're calling from, or **1**, followed by a number, followed by # to add a different number.

You're all set. Google Voice will now forward calls to the phone number you entered.

Another day, another hotel room. When it's time to check out of your hotel, you can turn off temporary call forwarding with these steps:

1. Call your Google number.

2. Press * and then enter your PIN if you're calling from a phone you haven't set up for forwarding with Google Voice, or just enter your PIN if you're calling from a phone that you've already set up for forwarding.

3. Press **4**. This lets you access the main settings menu.

4. Press **4** again. This lets you access your temporary settings.

5. Press **2**. This lets you set up a temporary forwarding number.

6. Press **3** to turn off your temporary forwarding number.

The phone you temporarily added will no longer ring when Google Voice receives a call for you.

Avoiding Unwanted Calls

So far, we've been talking about channeling incoming calls to your various phones, but there are probably some calls you'd rather avoid. You might not want to be called at certain times of the day, for example, or hear from certain callers. Or maybe you just feel like a little peace and quiet and you want to turn off calls altogether for a while.

Avoiding calls you don't want to answer is what this section is all about.

Setting a Ring Schedule

You probably don't need all of your registered phones to ring for every single call. For example, you may not want your home phone to ring during the hours you're at work. Google Voice lets you specify the times you'll allow certain phones to ring; this is called a *ring schedule*. Here's how to set a ring schedule for a phone:

1. Navigate to the Google Voice site.

2. Click the **Settings** link. This opens the Settings page.

3. Click the **Phones** tab. This tab displays the phones for which you've set up call forwarding.

4. Find the phone for which you want to set a ring schedule and click its **Edit** button. This opens that phone for editing.

5. Click the **Show Advanced Settings** link. The advanced settings list is shown in Figure 4.10.

6. Use the radio buttons to set a ring schedule for this phone. The options for the ring schedule are shown in Figure 4.10.

7. Click the **Save** button. Google Voice saves your settings.

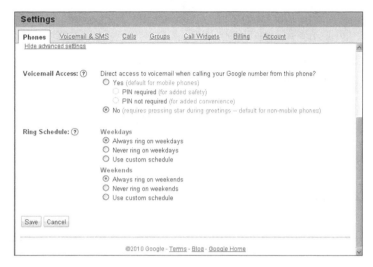

FIGURE 4.10   Setting a ring schedule.

Blocking a Specific Caller

When you don't want to hear from someone, you can tell Google Voice to
block that person's calls. (Or, if you prefer, you can always send that
caller directly to voicemail without causing any of your phones to ring.)
When you've blocked a caller and that person dials your Google Voice
number, the caller hears a message saying that the number is not in service. Google Voice prevents any of your phones from ringing and logs the
call as "blocked" in your call history.

> NOTE
> Blocked callers can't leave voicemail messages for you.

Here's how to block a specific caller:

1. Navigate to the Google Voice site.

2. Click the **Contacts** link. This opens the Contacts Manager.

3. Click the name of the contact you want to block.

4. Click the **Edit Google Voice Settings** link. This opens the contact's record for editing.

5. In the When This Contact Calls You section, click the **Edit** link. Here, you can specify which phones to ring when the contact calls you, as shown in Figure 4.11.

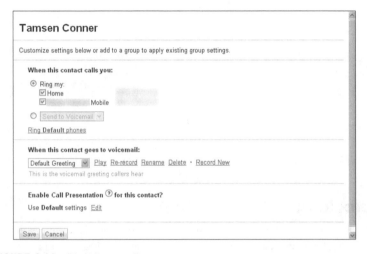

Tamsen Conner

Customize settings below or add to a group to apply existing group settings.

When this contact calls you:

⊙ Ring my:
  ☑ Home
  ☑   Mobile
○ Send to Voicemail ⌄
Ring **Default** phones

When this contact goes to voicemail:

Default Greeting ⌄   Play   Re-record   Rename   Delete · Record New
This is the voicemail greeting callers hear

Enable Call Presentation ⑦ **for this contact?**
Use **Default** settings   Edit

Save   Cancel

FIGURE 4.11   Blocking a caller.

6. Select the **Send to Voicemail** radio button.

> NOTE
>
> If you want to always send this contact straight to voicemail, you're done. Click **Save**. But if you want to block the contact from calling you at all, you've got another step.

7. Click the drop-down arrow in the Send to Voicemail box and select the **Block Caller** item.

8. Click the **Save** button.

If someone calls and leaves you a nasty message, you can also block that contact right from your Inbox. Click the down arrow next to the "more" link in the message and select the Block Caller from the drop-down list box.

Labeling Calls as Spam

You may know some people you don't want to block entirely, but you also don't want their messages to clutter up your Inbox. You can treat such callers as spammers, sending their calls to your Spam folder. That way, if you absolutely have to, you can check for the person's messages. (You access the Google Voice Spam folder by clicking the home page's left-hand Spam link.) But those messages won't land in your Inbox.

To label a caller as a spammer, follow these steps:

1. Navigate to the Google Voice site.

2. Click the **Contacts** link. This opens the Contacts Manager.

3. Click the contact's name you want to block.

4. Click the **Edit Google Voice Settings** link. This opens the contact's record for editing.

5. In the When This Contact Calls You section, click the **Edit** link. Here, you specify which phones to ring when the contact calls you.

6. Select the **Send to Voicemail** radio button.

7. In the Send to Voicemail box, click the drop-down arrow and select **Treat as Spam**.

8. Click the **Save** button.

Now, when the contact calls you, your phones will remain silent, the caller will go directly to voicemail, and any message left for you will be stored in your Spam folder.

TIP

If a spam message lands in your Inbox, you can also report it as spam from there. Check the offending message's left-hand checkbox and click the Report Spam button at the top of the Inbox page.

Do Not Disturb

When you need to focus on work or maybe take a quick nap, you don't want a ringing phone to interrupt. Google Voice's Do Not Disturb setting lets you temporarily route all calls to voicemail without ringing any of your phones. For a little peace and quiet, follow these steps:

1. Navigate to the Google Voice site.

2. Click the **Settings** link, which opens the Settings page.

3. Click the **Calls** tab. This displays the tab where you'll find the Do Not Disturb setting, as shown in Figure 4.12.

FIGURE 4.12   The Do Not Disturb setting.

4. In the Do Not Disturb section, click the **Enable "Do Not Disturb"** checkbox. This turns on the Do Not Disturb setting.

5. Click the **Save Changes** button.

And there you go—now you won't get any calls through Google Voice. To turn off the Do Not Disturb setting, just repeat the same steps, deselecting the **Enable "Do Not Disturb"** checkbox from step 4.

Summary

This lesson showed you the many options for answering calls made to your Google Voice number. Voicemail is one of those options—but there's a lot more you can do with Google Voice voicemail than we touched on here. In Lesson 5, "Using Voicemail." you'll see just how convenient and flexible voicemail can be.

LESSON 5

Using Voicemail

Google Voice voicemail capabilities far outstrip simple answering machines with its seemingly endless options. You can receive messages on the Web or using your phone. You can record custom greetings, set security using PINs, add notes to voicemails, restrict voicemail access by phone, send all calls to voicemail automatically (or send just specific callers to voicemail), and much more.

Welcome to Google Voicemail

If you've set up a Google Voice account, you've already got voicemail built in—how easy is that? Voicemail comes automatically with all Google Voice accounts.

By default, voicemail is enabled on your Google Voice phone number. So you don't have to lift a finger to set it up.

Using Google Voice Voicemail on a Mobile Phone

Mobile phone users can get all the benefits of the Google Voice voicemail system. That's right—you can set up your mobile phone to send voicemails directly to the Google Voice system.

Currently, this works only if your mobile phone is from one of these carriers:

- ▶ Alltel
- ▶ AT&T
- ▶ Cricket Wireless
- ▶ MetroPCS
- ▶ Sprint

▶ T-Mobile

▶ US Cellular

▶ Verizon

If you use one of these service providers, the first thing to do is add your mobile phone to Google Voice as a forwarding phone (click the **Settings** link, the **Phones** tab, and then click the **Add Another Phone** link). Once you've done that, follow these steps:

1. Navigate to the Google Voice site and log in (if necessary).

2. Click the **Settings** link to open the Settings page.

3. Click the **Phones** tab.

4. Click the **Activate Google Voicemail on This Phone** link for the mobile phone you want to give Google Voice voicemail access to. The dialog box shown in Figure 5.1 opens.

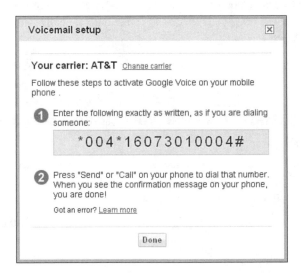

FIGURE 5.1   Activating a mobile phone for voicemail.

5. From your mobile phone, dial the number indicated in the dialog box.

6. Press **Call** or **Send** to make the call from your mobile phone.
   Google Voice answers and gives you a confirmation message.

You've now added your mobile phone to Google Voice and set it up to use
Google Voice voicemail. Read on to find out how to use all of those great
Google Voice voicemail features.

You've Got Voicemail!

When someone calls you on your Google Voice number (or on a mobile
phone you've assigned to Google Voice), the caller is prompted for his
name by default, and Google Voice calls your listed phones. If you don't
pick up, Google Voice informs the caller that you're not available with a
recorded message (you find out how to customize the message later in this
lesson) and asks him to "please leave a message after the tone." The standard answering machine beep then sounds.

At that point, your caller can leave a message and hang up. Great—you've
got voicemail. Now how do you pick it up?

There are two ways to pick up your voicemail—on the Web (using the
Google Voice site) and from a phone. We take a look at both in the following sections.

Receiving Voicemail on the Web

The first way to pick up your voicemail uses the Web and the Google
Voice site. By default, Google Voice sends you both the recording of the
caller's message and a transcript of that message.

Getting Voicemail Transcripts

Getting your voicemails on the Web is easy and takes just a couple of
steps:

1. Navigate to the Google Voice site and log in (if necessary).

2. Click the **Voicemail** link. Clicking the Voicemail link displays
   your voicemail, as shown in Figure 5.2. The transcript appears as
   shown in the figure.

FIGURE 5.2   Collecting voicemail.

> Using caller ID information, Google Voice indicates who called,
> so you see the name of the person calling you and his or her
> phone number or Unknown for callers who block caller ID.
>
> You can also click the **Inbox** link to see your voicemail, but
> you'll see all the messages and notifications you've received, not
> just your voicemails.

If you're picking up your voicemail from a mobile phone, use the Google
Voice mobile site instead, www.google.com/voice/m. This site appears in
Figure 5.3, and you can see the transcripts of your voicemails there.

Listening to Your Voicemail

You don't have to read transcribed voicemail messages; you can also listen
to the actual recording. That's useful if the transcript got messed up, if
you're not sure about the caller's tone, or if you just want to hear a loved
one's voice. To hear your voicemail using the Web, follow these steps:

1. Navigate to the Google Voice site and log in (if necessary).

2. Click the **Voicemail** link. Clicking the Voicemail link displays
   your voicemail.

   You can also click the **Inbox** link to see your voicemail, but
   you'll see all the messages and notifications you've received, not
   just your voicemails.

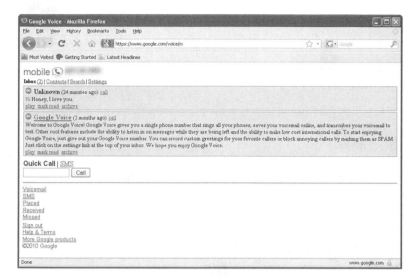

FIGURE 5.3   Collecting voicemail from the mobile site.

3. Click the box displaying a time and an arrow in the voicemail.
The voicemail plays.

If you're picking up your voicemail from a mobile phone, use the Google
Voice mobile site instead, www.google.com/voice/m. On the mobile site,
click the Play link in the voicemail you want to play.

Organizing Your Voicemail

If you get a lot of voicemails, clearing out a cluttered Inbox can be essential. You have three options here: archiving voicemails, marking them as
read, or deleting them.

When you archive a voicemail, that voicemail is removed from your
Inbox; from then on, it appears only when you click the Voicemail or
History link (the History link contains all the voicemail you ever
received). To archive a voicemail, just check the checkbox on the left in
the voicemail display and click the **Archive** button.

When you mark a voicemail as read, Google Voice remembers that you've
read it. You can then tell Google Voice *not* to display the voicemails
you've already read in the Inbox. Here's how:

1. Navigate to the Google Voice site and log in (if necessary).

2. Click the **Inbox** link to display the Inbox.

3. Check the checkbox on the left in every voicemail you want to mark as read.

4. Click the **Unread** button in the Show section above the Inbox. All of the voicemails you've marked as read disappear from the Inbox.

You can also delete voicemails. To do that, simply check the checkbox that appears on the left in the voicemail you want to delete and click the **Delete** button. Google Voice dumps that message in the Trash.

Sending Voicemail Notifications to a Different Email Address

By default, when you get a voicemail, Google Voice sends a notification to your registered email account and a text message to any mobile phone you've connected to your account. You can change the email address that receives email notifications.

Before you can change the email address, though, you need to tell Google Voice about the new email address. To do that, follow these steps:

1. Navigate to the Google Voice site and log in (if necessary).

2. Click the **Settings** link. Clicking the Settings link opens the Settings page.

3. Click the **SMS & Voicemail** tab. The tab SMS & Voicemail page appears.

4. Click the **Add a New Email Address** link. Doing so opens the page you can see in Figure 5.4.

5. Enter the new email address in the Add an Additional Email Address box.

6. Click the **Save** button. Google Voice sends a confirmation email to your new email address.

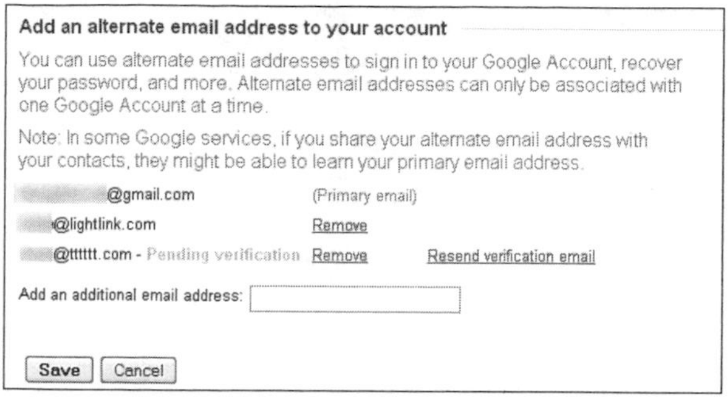

Add an alternate email address to your account

You can use alternate email addresses to sign in to your Google Account, recover your password, and more. Alternate email addresses can only be associated with one Google Account at a time.

Note: In some Google services, if you share your alternate email address with your contacts, they might be able to learn your primary email address.

@gmail.com   (Primary email)

@lightlink.com   Remove

@tttttt.com - Pending verification Remove   Resend verification email

Add an additional email address: [   ]

[Save] [Cancel]

FIGURE 5.4   Adding additional emails.

7. Click the link in the email from Google. Your browser opens. In the web page that appears, Google Accounts asks you for your password.

8. Enter your password.

9. Click the **Verify** button. Google Accounts displays an Associated Email Address Verified message, "Your new email address has been associated with your Google Voice account."

After you've told Google Voice about a particular email account, here's how you can have notifications sent there:

1. Navigate to the Google Voice site and log in (if necessary).

2. Click the **Settings** link. Clicking the Settings link opens the Settings page.

3. Click the **SMS & Voicemail** tab. Clicking this tab displays the page you see in Figure 5.5.

4. Select a new email address to send notifications to from the drop-down list box in the Voicemail Notifications section.

5. Click the **Save Changes** button. Your new email address is now set up.

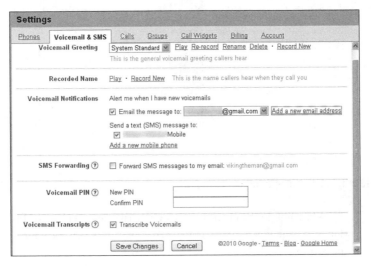

FIGURE 5.5   The SMS & Voicemail tab.

Receiving Voicemail on a Phone

Besides using the Web to pick up your voicemail, you can also use any
phone to hear your messages. To pick up your voicemail, call your
Google Voice number. Of course, there are different options to select from
and various choices to make, which we take a look at next.

Using Your PIN

When you set up your Google Voice account, you chose a PIN you could
use to get your voicemail. So when you call your Google Voice number,
you're asked to enter that PIN. Here's how it works:

1. Call your Google Voice number from any phone (including any
   phone you've set up for forwarding Google Voice calls to).

2. During the voicemail greeting, press the * key. Google Voice
   plays a beep.

3. Enter your four-digit PIN. Google Voice gives you a menu of
   prompts and tells you how many new voicemails you have.

4. Press **1** to hear your new voicemails. Google Voice plays the first new voicemail. After you listen, you get a menu of possible response keys to press:

   ▶ Press **2** to return the call.

   ▶ Press **7** to mark the message as read.

   ▶ Press **9** to keep the message as new.

   ▶ Press **4** for more options. When you press 4, you get this phone menu:

      ▶ Press **1** to play the voicemail again.

      ▶ Press **2** to return the call.

      ▶ Press **3** for voicemail details (time, date, and so on).

      ▶ Press **7** to mark the message as read.

      ▶ Press **8** to send a junk voicemail.

      ▶ Press **9** to keep the message as new.

   After you've made your choice, Google Voice then plays the next message and gives you the same options.

5. When you're done with your voicemails, hang up.

Connecting Directly to Voicemail

You can also tell Google Voice to connect you directly to voicemail when you call in (that's the default for mobile phones). That way, you don't have to press *, but you do still have to enter your PIN (unless you've told Google Voice not to ask for a PIN).

Here's how to make Google Voice connect you directly to voicemail when you call your Google number:

1. Navigate to the Google Voice site and log in (if necessary).

2. Click the **Phones** link to open the Phones page, which lists the phones you've told Google Voice about.

3. Click the **Edit** button for the phone you want to connect directly to voicemail.

4. Click the **Show Advanced Settings** link. Clicking this link
opens the settings you see in Figure 5.6.

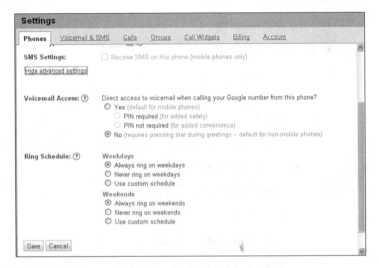

FIGURE 5.6   Advanced phone settings.

5. Select the **Yes** radio button in the Voicemail Access section to
connect the phone directly to voicemail.

6. Select the **PIN Required** or the **PIN Not Required** radio button
to specify whether or not you will be asked to enter your PIN
when you call your Google number. If you select PIN Not
Required, you will go directly to voicemail without hearing a
beep prompt for entering your PIN.

7. Click the **Save** button. Google Voice applies your settings.

Recording a Greeting

Google loves customization, so you probably won't be surprised to learn
that the Google Voice voicemail system can be fully customized, which
means you can customize the greetings people hear when they call you.
You can set up one greeting for your spouse, another for your best friend,
a different one for your mom, and a businesslike one for the boss. It's all
up to you.

There are several different ways to customize the greetings people hear when they go to voicemail—you can record just the name they hear, or you can do an entire greeting. You can also specify which callers get which messages.

Let's take a look at customizing the voicemail greeting now.

Recording the Name Callers Hear

You can record your name so that callers know whose voicemail they've reached. Recording your name in this way does not customize any part of the voicemail greeting besides your name.

Here's how to customize your name in Google Voice's voicemail greeting:

1. Navigate to the Google Voice site and log in (if necessary).

2. Click the **Settings** link, which opens the Settings page.

3. Click the **SMS & Voicemail** tab.

4. In the Recorded Name section, click **Record New**. A drop-down box appears with a list of your phones.

5. Select the phone you want Google Voice to use for recording your name and click **Connect.** Google Voice will call you on this phone so you can record your name.

6. Pick up the call.

7. At the prompt, say your name.

8. Hang up.

Recording a Custom Greeting

Recording your name is just the beginning—you can record an entire custom greeting. In fact, you can record many different greetings and select which one is active at any one time.

To record a custom greeting, follow these steps:

1. Navigate to the Google Voice site and log in (if necessary).

2. Click the **Settings** link to open the Settings page.

3. Click the **SMS & Voicemail** tab.

4. In the Voicemail Greeting section, click the **Record New** link.

5. In the dialog box that opens, enter a name for the greeting. Choose a name that describes the greeting, such as "General," "On vacation," or "Out of office."

6. Click **OK.**

7. When the Record Greeting dialog box opens, select the phone you want Google Voice to call you on and click **Connect.** Google Voice will call you on the phone you select so you can record your new greeting.

8. Answer the call.

9. At the prompt, say your new greeting.

10. Hang up.

Making a Recorded Greeting Active

After you've named and recorded a new greeting (such as "Happy Holidays"), you have to select that greeting so Google Voice will play it when callers reach your voicemail.

Here's how to make a particular greeting active:

1. Navigate to the Google Voice site and log in (if necessary).

2. Click the **Settings** link to open the Settings page.

3. Click the **SMS & Voicemail** tab. That tab opens, as shown in Figure 5.7.

4. In the Voicemail Greeting section, select the greeting you want to make active from the drop-down list box.

5. Click the **Save** button. Now, when a caller reaches your voicemail, Google Voice will play the greeting you selected.

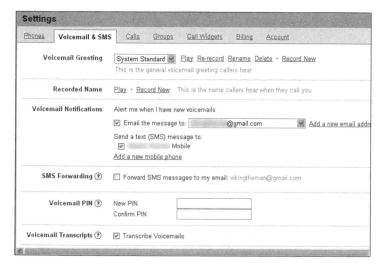

FIGURE 5.7 The SMS & Voicemail tab.

Selecting Which Greeting to Play by Caller

Here's a cool feature—you can actually specify which of your recorded voicemail greetings to use for which caller. That means you can play one greeting for work contacts, one for your spouse, another for the kids, and even one for the Boy Scout troop you head.

This feature works on a contact-by-contact basis—that is, you can select a greeting for each of your contacts.

> NOTE
>
> For this feature to work, you must have caller ID enabled for the contact, and the contact must be calling from a number that allows caller ID. Google Voice needs to verify which contact is calling before it can play the greeting you've specified for that contact.

Here's how to play a specific greeting for a particular contact:

1. Navigate to the Google Voice site and log in (if necessary).

2. Click the **Contacts** link to open the Contacts Manager.

3. Click the name of the contact you want to select a greeting for in the center column of the page. Clicking this link displays the contact's information.

4. Click the **Edit Google Voice Settings** link that appears beneath the contact's information. Google Voice opens the page you see in Figure 5.8.

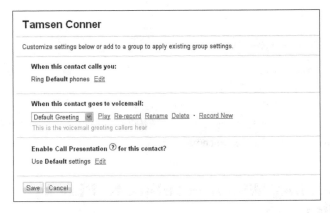

FIGURE 5.8   Editing a contact's information.

5. In the When This Contact Goes to Voicemail: section, use the drop-down list box to select the greeting you want this caller to hear when connected to voicemail.

NOTE

The drop-down box shows only the default greeting and any other greetings you've already recorded. If you haven't yet recorded any custom greetings, follow the steps given earlier in this chapter.

---

6. Click the **Save** button. Google Voice assigns the greeting you've selected to your contact.

Adding Notes to Voicemail

Have you ever scrambled for a pencil and a piece of paper so you could take notes on a voicemail as you listen? Google Voice makes that a thing of the past by letting you add notes to your voicemail transcripts. In other words, you can annotate voicemail transcripts, entering text to appear beneath the transcript itself.

Notes are useful in many situations—for example, imagine that your boss leaves you a message with a list of five things for you to do. You could add a note to the message and edit that note to keep track of your progress on the to-do list.

To add a note to a voicemail transcript, do this:

1. Navigate to the Google Voice site and log in (if necessary). Your Inbox is displayed.

2. Find the voicemail transcript you want, click the **More** link at the bottom, and select the **Add Note** menu item. A box appears where you can type in your note, as shown in Figure 5.9.

FIGURE 5.9 Adding a note to a transcript.

3. Enter the text of your note.

4. Click the **Save** button. The new note appears beneath the transcript, as shown in Figure 5.10.

You can edit the text of a note simply by clicking the note to open the text in an editing box. Make your changes and click the Save button to keep the changes you made.

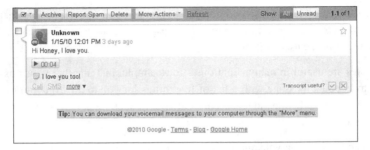

FIGURE 5.10   A new voicemail note.

Sharing Your Voicemail

You don't have to keep your voicemails to yourself. You can share them by emailing, downloading, or embedding them in web pages. This can come in handy when someone leaves a message you need to pass on to other people: a changed meeting time, for example, or some good news you want to share. You share voicemails by using the More menu that appears at the bottom of every voicemail.

Emailing a Voicemail

To email someone a voicemail, click the **More** menu at the bottom of the voicemail and select the **Email** menu item. When you do, Google Voice opens your email program and adds text to the email, including the link to the voicemail recording. If your registered email account is a Gmail account, Google Voice opens the dialog box you see in Figure 5.11.

> NOTE
>
> When you email someone a voicemail you've received, the email includes a link to the actual recording.

Fill in the rest of the email and click the **Send** button.

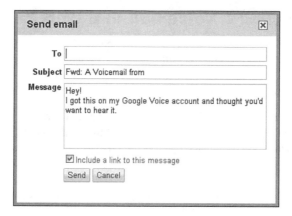

FIGURE 5.11 Emailing a voicemail.

Downloading a Voicemail

To download a voicemail recording, locate the voicemail you want, click its **More** link, and select the **Download** menu item that appears. Google Voice instructs your web browser to download the voicemail as an .mp3 recording, and your browser displays a dialog box something like the one you see in Figure 5.12 (depending on your browser).

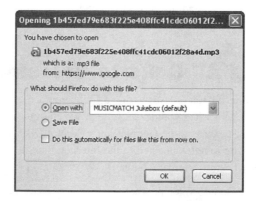

FIGURE 5.12 Downloading a voicemail.

Click **OK** to download the voicemail.

Embedding a Voicemail in a Web Page

The third way to share a voicemail is to embed it in a web page. That means putting HTML code into the web page to display a clickable control that will play the voicemail. So you can set up a web page where others can listen to the voicemail.

Where do you get that HTML code? Google Voice generates it for you. To get it, find the voicemail you want, click its **More** link, and select **Embed**. The HTML you need appears in a dialog box as shown in Figure 5.13.

FIGURE 5.13   Getting the HTML code to embed in a voicemail.

Copy that HTML code and insert it into the web page where you want to let others play the voicemail.

Sending All Calls to Voicemail

As you learned in Lesson 4, "Answering a Call," you can send all calls directly to voicemail when you need a little peace and quiet. That lesson showed you how to turn on the Google Voice Do Not Disturb setting from the website. If you're not connected to the Internet, though, you can also turn on Do Not Disturb from any phone:

1. Call your Google Voice number.

2. Press *. Google Voice responds with a beep prompt.

3. Enter your PIN. You hear the Google Voice phone menu.

4. Press **4** to access the main settings menu.

5. Press **4** again to access the temporary settings menu.

6. Press **1** to activate Do Not Disturb.

7. Press **1** to confirm your selection.

8. Hang up. Now, all incoming calls will go directly to voicemail, without ringing your phone.

The Do Not Disturb setting toggles on and off, so follow the same directions to turn it off again.

Turning Off Transcriptions

Transcribed voicemail messages are a key feature of Google Voice. But you may decide that you don't want transcribed messages emailed to you, that you prefer to hear recorded messages only. If that's the case, just follow these steps to turn off voicemail transcription:

1. Navigate to the Google Voice site and log in (if necessary).

2. Click the **Settings** link to open the Settings page.

3. Click the **SMS & Voicemail** tab. This opens the page where you can turn off voicemail transcription, as shown in Figure 5.14.

4. In the Voicemail Transcript section, deselect the **Transcribe Voicemails** checkbox.

5. Click the **Save Changes** button.

And that's it—Google Voice will no longer transcribe your voicemails. Of course, you can still listen to your recorded voicemail messages as usual.

If you change your mind and want those transcribed messages to start appearing in your Inbox again, you can enable voicemail transcripts at any time. Repeat steps 1–3, but in step 4, select the **Transcribe Voicemails** checkbox and then click **Save Changes**. You've turned voicemail transcription back on.

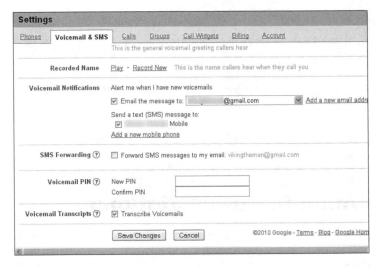

FIGURE 5.14   Turning off voicemail transcription.

Summary

In this Lesson, you mastered using voicemail with Google Voice. As you continue to send and receive calls with Google Voice, your list of contacts will grow. Lesson 6, "Working with Contacts and Groups," teaches you how to work with contacts and groups, which let you gather related contacts and manage them all at once.

LESSON 6

Working with Contacts and Groups

The more contacts you add to Google Voice, the more you need to organize them. For example, say your contacts include 30 friends, your extended family of 20 relatives, and 55 coworkers. That's a lot of people. To make managing multiple contacts easier, Google Voice lets you work with *groups*. A group is simply a set of contacts for which you can specify all settings at once. So when you record a new voicemail greeting and want to apply it to specific contacts—such as all family members ("It's my birthday, please list the items you intend to give me.") or all coworkers ("I'm on vacation: emergencies only!")—you can put those contacts into a group and quickly and easily assign the relevant voicemail greeting to everyone in the group. But that's just the start of what you can do with groups and contacts. This lesson shows you how to work with contacts and groups to fine-tune how Google Voice handles your calls.

Personalizing Contacts

After creating a contact (see Lesson 3, "Making a Call"), you can customize a contact's settings by choosing what greeting a contact gets in voicemail, which phones to ring, and so on.

Next we look at the various ways to work with contacts, ramping up your expertise on the subject. When you've mastered contacts and what they can do, we organize those contacts into groups.

Editing a Contact's Settings

You can customize a contact's settings by setting what greeting a contact gets in voicemail, what phones ring when the contact calls, and whether or not to use Call Presentation (call screening) for this contact. You select a contact's customization settings by following these steps:

1. Navigate to the Google Voice site and log in (if necessary). The Google Voice site appears in your browser.

2. Click the **Contacts** link to open the Contacts Manager.

3. In the Contacts Manager's center column, select the name of the contact you want to customize. The contact's information appears in the right column.

4. Click the **Edit Google Voice Settings** link. Doing so opens the page you see in Figure 6.1.

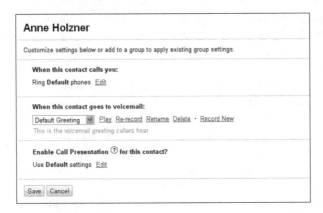

FIGURE 6.1   The Edit Google Voice Settings page for a contact.

Here are the settings you can modify:

▶ Select which phones to ring when this contact calls.

▶ Select the greeting that's played when the contact goes to voicemail.

▶ Enable or disable Call Presentation for this contact (that is, turn call screening on or off).

5. Make the changes you wish to customize Google Voice for this contact.

6. Click the **Save** button.

Deleting a Contact

Some contacts will change with time—coworkers leave your company, friends move away, or you might just decide you need to trim your contacts list. When these situations arise, you can delete a contact.

Adding a contact is easy (see Lesson 3), but you should know that when you delete a contact, that contact is gone. If you made a mistake or you want to reinstate a deleted contact, you'll have to create that contact from scratch. So think before you delete.

If you do want to delete a contact, here's what you do:

1. Navigate to the Google Voice site and log in (if necessary). The Google Voice site appears in your browser.

2. Click the **Contacts** link to open the Contacts Manager.

3. In the Contacts Manager's center column, select the name of the contact you want to delete. The contact's information appears in the right column.

4. Click the upper-right **Delete Contact** button.

   A dialog box appears and asks, "Are you sure you want to delete this contact? Deleting this contact will delete it from other Google apps you may use like Picasa, Reader, Google Chat, Latitude, Google Voice, Mobile Sync (including iPhones and Android), and Gmail autocomplete. This action cannot be undone."

> TIP
>
> Before you delete a contact, stop and think. If you need to stay in touch with this contact for one of Google's other applications or services, like Gmail or the Picasa photo-sharing service, don't delete the contact from Google Voice.

5. Click **OK** in the dialog box to delete the contact. The contact is then gone from Google Voice (and the other applications noted in step 4).

Importing a Contact from Your Inbox

If a contact leaves a voicemail, and Google Voice recognizes the number from caller ID, it puts the contact's name at the top of the message you get in your Inbox.

But what if someone calls you who's not a contact already? In that case, Google Voice puts the number at the top of the message that appears in the Inbox, as you can see in Figure 6.2.

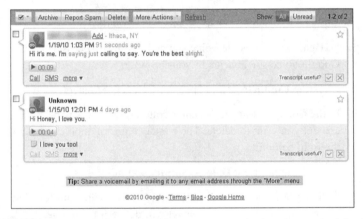

FIGURE 6.2 A voicemail message from someone who is not a contact (top).

Is there an easy way to make that person a contact? You bet—just follow these steps:

1. Navigate to the Google Voice site and log in (if necessary).

2. Look in your Inbox for the message you want and find the number at its top. Click the **Add** link immediately to the number's right. When you click the Add link, a Quick Add drop-down box appears, as shown in Figure 6.3.

> NOTE
> The Add link appears only for people who are not already contacts.

3. Enter the new contact's name in the Name box.

FIGURE 6.3   The Quick Add box.

4. Select the type of phone the new contact called on—Mobile, Work, or Home—from the drop-down list in the Quick Add box.

5. Click the **Create/Add** button.

And that's all you need to do—Google Voice adds the person who called you to your list of contacts.

Searching Your Contacts

If you have a large number of contacts, congratulate yourself on your popularity. But a huge list of contacts can become unwieldy—try scrolling through a list of a hundred contacts, and you'll see the problem. You can make contacts easier to find by letting Google Voice search your contacts for you. (And Google knows how to search!)

Here's how:

1. Navigate to the Google Voice site and log in (if necessary).

2. Click the **Contacts** link to open the Contacts Manager.

3. Find the search box (it's above the Contacts Manager's center column and shows a magnifying glass) and type in your search term; press **Enter**. Google Voice searches all contacts for your search term and displays any matches in the center column, as you can see in Figure 6.4.

4. Click the name of the contact you want in the search results. The Contacts Manager displays that contact's information.

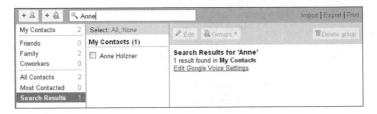

FIGURE 6.4   Search results.

> **TIP**
>
> When you're searching for a contact, you can search using all or part of the contact's name.

Importing Contacts

If your email or other program lets you export your address or phone book into a .csv (comma-separated value) file, you can import those contacts directly into Google Voice. First, you need to open the other program and save its contacts as a .csv file. (Check the program's Help files if you're not sure how to do that.) Make a note of where you've saved the file.

Then, to import the .csv file into Google Voice, follow these steps:

1. Navigate to the Google Voice site and log in (if necessary).

2. Click the **Contacts** link to open the Contacts Manager.

3. In the Contacts Manager's upper right section, click **Import**. A dialog box appears that allows you to import your contacts.

4. Click the **Browse** button in the dialog box, navigate to the .csv file, and select it.

5. Click the **Import** button. Google Voice imports your contacts.

Now you've brought all the contact info you've collected in the other program into Google Voice.

All About Groups

As mentioned at the beginning of this chapter, groups let you organize your contacts, making it easy to apply a single setting to a number of contacts at once. So, for example, you can specify which group—everyone in your Friends group or your Family group, for example—gets which voicemail greeting.

Your Google Voice account comes with several groups already built-in:

- ▶ Friends

- ▶ Family

- ▶ Coworkers

You can add contacts to any of those groups with just a few clicks. In fact, any contact can be added to any of those groups—just one or all three if you prefer.

Google Voice's built-in groups will sort many of your contacts, but as you see in a bit, you can create your own groups, too. For example, you might want a special group to hold all contacts for the PTA, your garden club, or your softball team. This section shows you how.

In the meantime, let's see how to add contacts to an existing group.

Adding a Contact to an Existing Group

Adding contacts to the groups that come with Google Voice (Friends, Family, or Coworkers) is simple. Just follow these steps:

1. Navigate to the Google Voice site and log in (if necessary).

2. Click the **Contacts** link to open the Contacts Manager.

3. In the Contacts Manager's center column, select all the contacts you want to add to an existing group by checking the checkboxes next to their names.

4. In the right column, click the **Groups** button. A menu appears, displaying a list of groups you can add contacts to or remove them from.

5. Select the group you want to add the contacts to. Google Voice adds the contacts you've selected to the group you chose and updates the total number of members in the group in the second column of the Contacts Manager. For example, you can see that two contacts were added to the Family group in Figure 6.5.

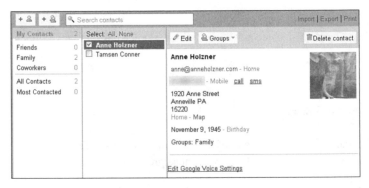

FIGURE 6.5   Adding two contacts to the Family group.

Accessing Group Members

Now that you've added contacts to a group, you may be wondering how you access those contacts. In other words, what if you want to see all of the contacts in a certain group? Nothing to it:

1. Navigate to the Google Voice site and log in (if necessary).

2. Click the **Contacts** link to open the Contacts Manager.

3. Under My Contacts in the second column from the left, click the name of the group you want to access. The group opens in the column immediately to the right of the groups column, listing the selected group's contacts, as shown in Figure 6.6.

    Now you have access to all of the members of the selected group.

4. Click the name of the contact in the center column of the Contacts Manager to open that contact's page. This displays that individual contact's information in the right column, as shown in Figure 6.7.

FIGURE 6.6   Selecting a group.

FIGURE 6.7   A contact's information.

Deleting Contacts from a Group

It can be hard to say goodbye. But after you've managed that, it's easy to delete any contact from a group. Say, for example, that a coworker has left the company, and you want to remove that contact from your Coworkers group. You can delete a contact from a group by doing this:

1. Navigate to the Google Voice site and log in (if necessary).

2. Click the **Contacts** link to open the Contacts Manager.

3. Under My Contacts in the second column from the left, click the name of the group that contains the contact you want to remove. Google Voice displays the group's contacts in the column immediately to the right of the groups column.

4. Find the contact you want to remove and check its checkbox. (You can remove more than one contact at a time by selecting the checkboxes for each contact you want to remove.)

5. In the right column, click the **Groups** button. A drop-down menu appears.

6. In the drop-down menu, find the Remove From heading. Beneath it, select the name of the group you want to remove the contact from. Google Voice removes the contact(s) you chose from the group.

NOTE

Removing a contact from a group does *not* delete that contact from Google Voice. To get rid of a contact for good, see "Deleting a Contact" earlier in this lesson.

Creating a Group from Scratch

As you've seen, Google Voice comes with three groups built right in: Friends, Family, and Coworkers. But you can add your own groups, as well.

For example, you might belong to a book club that reads and discusses novels. You can set up a group for that club and call it something like Reading Group.

You can create such a new group easily if you follow these steps:

1. Navigate to the Google Voice site and log in (if necessary).

2. Click the **Contacts** link to open the Contacts Manager.

3. Click the **New Group** button. When you click the New Group button, a dialog box opens, asking, "What would you like to name this group?"

4. Enter the name of the new group into the dialog box.

5. Click **OK**.

New Group button

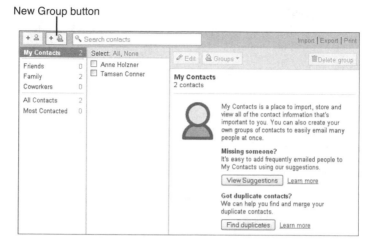

FIGURE 6.8   Creating a new group.

Following these steps creates the new group, "Reading Group" in our example, and adds it to the list of groups, as you can see in Figure 6.9. Now that you've created the group, you can add contacts to it, as explained earlier in this lesson.

FIGURE 6.9   A new group.

Creating a Group by Adding Contacts

Instead of going through the two-step process of creating a group from scratch and then finding and adding contacts to it, you can save yourself a step by selecting the contacts who'll be in the new group and setting up a group just for them. Here's how:

1. Navigate to the Google Voice site and log in (if necessary).

2. Click the **Contacts** link to open the Contacts Manager.

3. In the center column listing your contacts, select the contacts who'll be in the new group. To select a contact, check the checkbox beside the contact's name.

4. In the right column, click the Groups button. A drop-down menu appears.

5. From the drop-down list, under the Add To heading, select **New Group**. A dialog box opens, asking, "What would you like to name this group?"

6. Enter the name of the new group into the dialog box.

7. Click **OK**. Google Voice creates the new group, already populated with the contacts you selected.

Customizing Forwarding for a Group

You can have all calls from the members of a group automatically forwarded to one or more phones. This comes in handy when you want, for example, all work calls to come in on one phone.

To set up call forwarding options for a group, follow these steps:

1. Navigate to the Google Voice site and log in (if necessary).

2. Click the **Contacts** link to open the Contacts Manager.

3. Click the name of the group for which you want to set call forwarding options. The group opens in the Contacts Manager.

4. Click the **Edit Google Voice Settings** link. Clicking this link opens the settings for all groups, as you can see in Figure 6.10.

5. Click the **Edit** button for the group whose settings you want to change. This opens the settings for the particular groups you're interested in, as you can see in Figure 6.11.

6. In the "When people in this group call you" section, click the **Edit** link. You see a list of forwarding phones that you've set up with Google Voice.

7. Put checkmarks in front of the phones that you want to receive the forwarded calls.

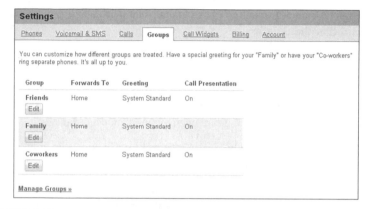

FIGURE 6.10   Editing all groups' settings.

FIGURE 6.11   Editing a group's settings.

8. Click the **Save** button.

And that's it—now when people from that group call you, their calls will ring the phone(s) you've indicated.

Customizing a Greeting for a Group

You can also select which greeting the members of a group hear when they go to voicemail. For example, you might want a more formal sounding message for contacts in your Clients group than you'd want for your friends.

To select which voicemail greeting contacts in a particular a group will hear, follow these steps:

1. Navigate to the Google Voice site and log in (if necessary).

2. Click the **Contacts** link to open the Contacts Manager.

3. Click the name of the group for which you want to set call forwarding options. The group opens in the Contacts Manager.

4. Click the **Edit Google Voice Settings** link. Clicking this link opens the settings for all groups.

5. Click the **Edit** button for the group whose settings you want to change. This opens the settings for the particular groups you're interested in.

6. In the "When people in this group go to voicemail" section, use the default drop-down list box to select the greeting you want to play.

7. Click the **Save** button. Google Voice saves your choice.

Now, when any member of that group goes to voicemail, that person will hear the greeting you selected.

Customizing Call Presentation for a Group

What does it mean to customize Call Presentation for a group? It means that you can turn Google Voice's call screening options on or off for members of the group. Call Presentation asks the caller to announce his or her name so that Google Voice can pass it on to you when you answer the phone.

For example, you might not want Call Presentation for family members— you're happy for Google Voice to put those callers straight through. So you may want to turn off Call Presentation for contacts in your Family group.

> NOTE
> Lesson 4, "Answering a Call," explains Call Presentation.

Here's how to turn Call Presentation on or off for an entire group:

1. Navigate to the Google Voice site and log in (if necessary).

2. Click the **Contacts** link to open the Contacts Manager.

3. Click the name of the group for which you want to set call forwarding options. This opens that group in the Contacts Manager.

4. Click the **Edit Google Voice Settings** link. Clicking this link opens the settings for all groups.

5. Click the **Edit** button for the group whose settings you want to change. This opens the settings for the particular groups you're interested in.

6. In the Enable Call Presentation section, select one of these radio buttons:

   ▶ Default (use the default for Call Presentation)

   ▶ On

   ▶ Off

7. Click the **Save** button. Google Voice enables or disables Call Presentation (as you chose) for all members of the group.

Deleting a Group

Groups can be temporary—for example, you might have a group set up to arrange for a special event, like a fund raiser. When the event is done, you can delete the group.

Here's how to delete a group:

1. Navigate to the Google Voice site and log in (if necessary).

2. Click the **Contacts** link to open the Contacts Manager.

3. Click the name of the group you want to delete. The group opens in the Contact Manager's right column.

4. Click the upper-right **Delete Group** button. A dialog box appears with the message, "Are you sure you want to delete the group [*name of group*]? This action cannot be undone."

5. Click **OK** to delete the group. The group disappears from the groups list.

And that's it—the group is gone (if you want it back, you'll have to create it again from scratch).

> NOTE
>
> Deleting a group doesn't delete the contacts who belong to that group. They're still contacts; they just no longer belong to the group you eliminated.

Summary

Creating groups makes managing your contacts a lot easier, as you saw in this lesson. In Lesson 7, "Text Messaging," you'll move beyond voice calls and learn how to send and receive text messages through Google Voice.

LESSON 7

Text Messaging

Text messaging, also called *texting*, has become one of the most popular forms of communication in recent years. Sending and receiving text messages using Google Voice is free (that's for domestic text messages—international text messaging isn't yet available), and you can read messages through your Google Voice Inbox or your email account.

PLAIN ENGLISH   **SMS**

The official name for texting is SMS, which stands for *Short Message Service*. SMS is becoming something of a misnomer as text messages get longer and longer. Originally hampered by the method of text-entry—on some phones, you have to press keys multiple times to access certain characters—text messages have become easier to compose and send because many mobile phones now come with complete keyboards.

Sending a Text Message

For many people with mobile phones, sending text messages is a bit of a hassle. If your phone has a standard keypad (with no keyboard), for example, you have to press 9 four times to enter the letter z. And let's not even talk about what it takes to switch from lowercase to uppercase or enter a number.

And what if you don't have a mobile phone at all? You can't send text messages over a landline. Does that mean you're stranded textless in a world of SMS?

Google Voice comes to the rescue on both counts. You can send text messages using Google Voice just by typing on your computer's keyboard—what could be easier?

> NOTE
>
> Like Shakespeare, Google Voice believes that brevity is the soul of wit. When you send a text message through Google Voice, you're allowed a maximum of 160 characters for your message.

Let's give it a try.

Using the SMS Button

When you sign in to Google Voice, you see the familiar Call button at upper left. And beside it is a button marked SMS.

You can use the SMS button to send text messages—and we'll do that here. But note that the SMS button is only one of the ways you can send text messages from Google Voice. You'll learn the others as we proceed.

> NOTE
>
> You have to use the web interface to send text messages—there's no way to send them through your Google Voice number yet.

To compose and send a text message from the Google Voice website, just follow these steps:

1. Navigate to the Google Voice site and log in (if necessary).

2. Click the **SMS** button. Clicking this button opens the drop-down box you see in Figure 7.1.

3. Enter the number of the mobile phone you want to receive your text message.

4. Type in your text message. Remember that you're limited to a maximum of 160 characters per message. To help you keep track, Google Voice keeps a running tally above the text box as you type, letting you know how many characters you have left.

5. Click the **Send** button.

And that's it—your text message is on its way. Simple, eh?

FIGURE 7.1   The SMS button's drop-down box.

Using Your Contacts List

You have more options for sending a text message than using the SMS button. You can also send text messages to your contacts easily.

For example, take a look at the contact information in the right column in Figure 7.2. To the right of the contact's mobile phone number is an "sms" link. We put it to work here.

FIGURE 7.2   A contact's information.

To send an SMS message to any contact, follow these steps:

1. Navigate to the Google Voice site and log in (if necessary).

2. Click the **Contacts** link to open the Contacts Manager.

3. Select the name of the contact you want to receive a text message. This opens that contact's information, such as in the example you see in Figure 7.2.

4. Click the **SMS** link. The dialog box you see in Figure 7.3 opens.

FIGURE 7.3   Sending an SMS to a contact.

5. Enter your text message. Remember that you're limited to a maximum of 160 characters per message. To help you keep track, Google Voice keeps a running tally above the text box as you type, letting you know how many characters you have left.

6. Click the **Send** button.

TIP

Is there a way to send a text message to all members of a group at once? No, not at this writing—if you want to send a text message to multiple contacts, you've got to send it to each one individually. Perhaps in the future, Google Voice will allow you to send text messages en masse to all the members of a group, but not yet.

Replying to a Voicemail

Here's another easy way to send a text message—you can simply reply to a voicemail.

But this method has a catch—the caller must have called from a mobile phone when leaving the voicemail. (That's because only mobile phones can receive text messages.) For example, take a look at Figure 7.4. The top voicemail was left from a mobile phone. At the bottom of that voicemail message is an active SMS link.

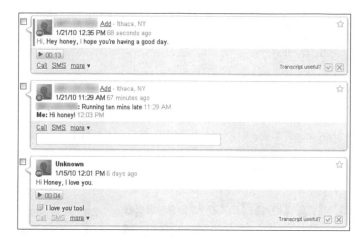

FIGURE 7.4   The SMS link in a voicemail.

In contrast, the voicemail at the bottom of the page came in from a land-line phone. For that message, the SMS link is grayed out, which means you can't reply to that voicemail with a text message.

To send a text message in reply to a voicemail left from a mobile phone, follow these steps:

1. Navigate to the Google Voice site and log in (if necessary).

2. Find the voicemail you want to reply to and click its **SMS** link. As noted, the voicemail must have been left from a mobile phone for the SMS link to be active.

   Clicking the link opens a text box, as you can see in Figure 7.5.

FIGURE 7.5   Replying to a voicemail.

3. Enter your text message. Remember that you're limited to a maximum of 160 characters per message (note the tally provided above the text box).

4. Click the **Send** button.

Your SMS message is on its way.

Using the Google Voice interface makes it quick and easy to reply to voicemails you've received—and the same goes for replying to text messages, as we're about to see.

Replying to a Text Message

When someone sends you a text message, he or she probably expects you to reply with a text message of your own. Using Google Voice, you can.

For example, take a look at Figure 7.6. In this example, the message at the top of the Inbox is a text message sent from a mobile phone to a Google Voice number. When you receive a text message in this way, you can reply immediately with another text message.

FIGURE 7.6   A text message in the Inbox.

1. Navigate to the Google Voice site and log in (if necessary).

2. Click the **SMS** link in the text message you want to reply to. As noted, the text message must have been left from a mobile phone for the SMS link to be active.

Clicking the link opens a text box, as you can see in Figure 7.7.

FIGURE 7.7 Replying to a text message.

3. Enter your text message (160-character limit).

4. Click the **Send** button.

As you can see, when someone sends a text message to your Google Voice number, it's simple to reply in kind.

Receiving Text Messages

As you've just seen, even if you've never sent a text message before, with Google Voice you'll soon be sending them like a pro. It's that easy. Now let's turn to what Google Voice really excels at—receiving text messages.

There's a variety of ways you can get text messages sent through Google Voice—on your mobile phone, in your Inbox, via email, and so on. With all those options, you never have to miss an urgent text message.

> NOTE
>
> If you read your text messages in your Google Voice Inbox or through your email account, it doesn't cost you a dime. If you read them on your cell phone, of course, your carrier's normal charges apply.

Let's take a look at all the possibilities.

> NOTE
>
> Google Voice won't let you pick up your text messages from a non-mobile phone. You might expect that a service that transcribes your phone messages into text could go the other way and read your text messages to you over the phone—and perhaps it will in the future, but not yet.

Getting Text Messages in Your Inbox

By default, Google Voice delivers text messages to your Inbox, where they're easy to read and organize.

Here's how to retrieve a text message from your Inbox:

1. Navigate to the Google Voice site and log in (if necessary).

2. Click the **Inbox** link. Clicking the Inbox link opens your Inbox.

3. Locate the text message icon in the Inbox to find your text messages. The text message icon shows a human figure (or, if you've gotten uploaded a photo of that contact, the icon shows the photo); in the foreground is a small circle with three horizontal white lines, meant to symbolize lines of text, as shown in Figure 7.8.

FIGURE 7.8 The text message icon.

4. To call the sender of the text message back, click the **Call** link; to text them back, click the **SMS** link. When you receive a text message in your Inbox, you can reply either by calling the sender or by texting him back. When you click the SMS link, you proceed as described in the previous section of this chapter.

Keeping Track of Your Text Messages

The Inbox holds a lot of information. It stores text messages, but it also stores voicemails and other messages. If you're looking for a text message, it can be confusing to sort through all those different kinds of messages. Is there some way to organize just your text messages?

Yes, there is. Google Voice has a separate inbox dedicated to your SMS messages. To see how that works, follow these steps:

1. Navigate to the Google Voice site and log in (if necessary).

2. Click the **SMS** link at left in Google Voice (not the SMS button). Clicking the SMS link opens your inbox for text messages, as Figure 7.9 shows.

FIGURE 7.9   Your text messages.

3. To manage your text messages, click the **More** link at the bottom of any text message, which gives you these options:

   ▶ Mark as read

   ▶ Add note

   ▶ Block caller

4. To move the text message to the Inbox, check the checkbox to the left of the text message; click the **Move to Inbox** button.

5. To delete the text message, check the checkbox to the left of the text message; click the **Delete** button.

6. To call the sender back, click the text message's **Call** link.

7. To text the sender back, click the text message's **SMS** link.

Forwarding Your SMS Messages to Email

You can forward your text messages to an email account. And here's the cool thing: When you get a text message via email, you can reply to it and your reply will be sent as a text message back to the original sender. So even if you prefer using email to texting, you can send a reply using email and the recipient gets it as a text message.

To forward text messages to your default email account, you must enable Google Voice to send text messages to that email account. Doing that takes just a few quick steps:

1. Navigate to the Google Voice site and log in (if necessary).

2. Click the **Settings** link, which opens the Settings page in your browser.

3. Select the **SMS & Voicemail** tab. This tab is where you set up
   email forwarding for text messages, and it appears in Figure
   7.10.

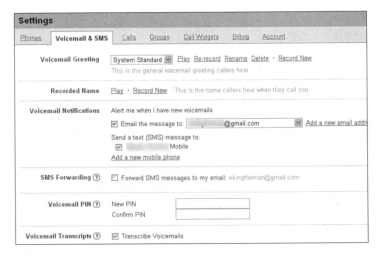

FIGURE 7.10 Google Voice Settings.

4. In the SMS Forwarding section, check the box next to **Forward
   SMS Messages to My Email**. This tells Google Voice to send
   your text messages on to your default email account.

5. Click the **Save Changes** button. Google Voice saves your new
   setting.

And you've done it—now Google Voice will forward received text messages to your email address. When you can reply to a text message from
your email account, the reply gets sent as a text message (so remember to
limit your reply to 160 characters or fewer).

Using an email account to receive and reply to text messages is a particularly useful feature if you have a keypad-only phone that makes it arduous
to send SMS messages (press 9 four times for z, and so on). And here's
another bonus: The text messages you send through Google Voice are
free.

Of course, receiving and replying to text messages using your email
account means that you must have access to a computer to read and

answer those text messages—and that won't always be the case. But if
you've registered a mobile phone with your Google Voice account, you
can still get text messages on that phone. (You don't have to turn off email
forwarding to receive text messages on your phone.) So whether you're
online or off, Google Voice has you covered.

TIP

When using email forwarding, you can reply to an SMS text message
only from the same email address that received the message. This
becomes an issue if you set up email forwarding from the email
address you registered with Google Voice to another email account.
For example, say that Google Voice forwards received text messages
to your work email address. Then, while you're away from the office
for a few days, you set up your work account to forward emails to
your personal email account. When someone sends a text message
to your Google Voice number, Google Voice forwards it to your work
email address as usual—but then your work email account forwards
it to your personal email address. For your reply to be sent as an
SMS text message, you need to reply from your registered Google
Voice email address (your work address in the example)—*not* from
the address your registered account forwarded the message to.

You're not stuck with your registered email address as the only one that
can receive text messages. To change the email account to which Google
Voice forwards text messages, take a look at the next topic.

Changing the Email Address Where You Receive Text Messages

As you've seen, you can tell Google Voice to forward any text messages
you receive to your email address. If you want, you can change the email
address that gets your text messages. Here's how to do that:

1. Navigate to the Google Voice site and log in (if necessary).

2. Click the **Settings** link, which opens the Settings page.

3. Click the **SMS & Voicemail** tab.

4. In the Voicemail Notifications section, use the drop-down list box
   to select a new email address to receive forwarded text messages.

5. Click the **Save Changes** button. Google Voice will now forward received text messages to the email address you've chosen.

What if the email address you want doesn't appear in the drop-down list box? You can add it by following these steps:

1. Navigate to the Google Voice site and log in (if necessary).

2. Click the **Settings** link.

3. Click the **SMS & Voicemail** tab.

4. Click the **Add a New Email Address** link. Google Voice displays the Add an Additional Email Address box.

5. In the Add an Additional Email Address box, type in the new email address.

6. Click the **Save** button. To make sure you've entered a valid email address, Google Voice sends a confirmation email to the address you submitted.

7. Open your email program and find the email from Google Voice; click the confirmation link. Your web browser opens a Google Accounts sign-in page that asks for your password.

8. Enter your password.

9. Click the **Verify** button. Google accounts displays a page with the words "Associated Email Address Verified."

Your new email address has been associated with your Google Voice account. Now you can use that address to receive and reply to text messages.

International SMS

There's not much to say yet about the topic of getting and sending international text messages in Google Voice. As of now, you can't do it. That is, you can't send or receive SMS messages from international phone numbers because Google Voice currently doesn't support that ability.

That's a pity if you have international contacts, of course. But as Lesson 9, "Billing and International Calls," explains, Google Voice does let you *call* international numbers cheaply. As Google Voice grows in popularity, international text messaging may be added in the future. If that happens, you might have to pay a fee to send international text messages (sending domestic text messages costs nothing). But only time will tell.

What's That 406 Area Code?

When you send a text message through Google Voice, that message appears to come from your Google Voice number. In other words, the person who receives the message sees that it came from your Google Voice number. Make sure, then, that your friends, family, and other contacts know your Google Voice number. Otherwise, they might think the message from an unfamiliar number is junk and delete it unread.

It works the other way, too: When someone sends you a text message from a Google Voice phone, that person's Google Voice number appears as the message's sender. For example, say you have a friend who has a Google Voice number. When your friend sends you a text message, the message appears to come from their Google Voice number, and you can text them back at that number.

So far, so good. But what if someone texts you from a *non*-Google Voice mobile phone? If they text your Google Voice number, the text message appears in your Inbox, and the number listed is the person's actual mobile phone number. In other words, if your sister, who doesn't have a Google Voice account, texts you at your Google Voice number, her text message appears in your Inbox, listing her actual mobile phone number.

Now, however, what happens if you have call forwarding turned on to forward your calls—including text messages—to a mobile phone? If a person with a Google Voice number texts you, their Google Voice number appears in your mobile phone as the sender of the text message.

Still with me? Here's where it gets tricky—and here's where the 406 area code comes in. If someone texts you from a non-Google Voice mobile phone and Google Voice forwards that text message to your mobile phone, the number that appears with the text message will *not* be the sender's actual mobile phone number.

In this case, the number that appears in your mobile phone has a 406 area code. Wait a minute—isn't 406 the area code for the state of Montana?

Yup—but it's also the area code that Google Voice uses to relay SMS messages. That's so that when you text the person back, your text message is sent through Google Voice, and the number that appears in the person's phone is your Google Voice number.

If it had just been the number of the sender's mobile phone that appeared in your mobile phone, then when you texted back, your message would go directly from your phone—*not* through Google Voice. That's why Google uses numbers from the 406 area code—so when you reply to text messages that were forwarded to your mobile phone through Google Voice, the original sender sees your reply as though it's coming from your Google Voice number.

So don't let the 406 area code confuse you. It's just a relay number that Google uses to make sure your Google Voice number shows up as the sender when you reply to a text message.

Whew.

Blocking Unwanted Text Messages

Ever get an annoying text message and wish you could block the sender from ever contacting you again? Guess what. You can with Google Voice. To block a caller from sending you text messages, follow these steps:

1. Navigate to the Google Voice site and log in (if necessary).

2. Click the **Inbox** link. Clicking this link opens your text messages for reading. If you prefer, you can click the SMS link to see just your text messages.

3. Find a text message from the caller you want to block and click its **More** link. A drop-down list box appears.

4. Click **Block Caller**. This opens the dialog box you see in Figure 7.11, which asks if you're sure you want to block this person from sending you text messages.

5. Click **Block**. The person can no longer contact you through Google Voice.

FIGURE 7.11 Blocking a caller.

> **NOTE**
>
> Blocking a caller blocks that person from both calling and texting you.

If you change your mind, you can unblock a caller:

1. Navigate to the Google Voice site and log in (if necessary).

2. Click the **History** link. Clicking this link opens all the text messages and calls you've received.

3. Find a text message or voicemail from the caller you want to unblock and click its **More** link. A drop-down list box appears.

4. Click **Unblock Caller**. Now the person can use Google Voice to call you and send you text messages.

Reporting Text Messages as Spam

Spam is everywhere—and that includes in your Inbox. If you get on a spammer's list, you could be flooded with spam text messages.

> TIP
>
> Avoid Internet sites that promise "free" ring tone downloads. Many of these sites are set up to harvest mobile phone numbers—you have to enter your number to get the ring tone—and send them unsolicited advertising. Such sites word their Terms of Service to make this practice legal; once you're on the list, it's difficult to stop the spam. That's where Google Voice can help.

Google Voice is very good about suppressing spam. Just let Google Voice know that a message is spam, and Google stops it from reaching your phone.

To report a text message as spam, follow these steps:

1. Navigate to the Google Voice site and log in (if necessary).

2. Click the **Inbox** link. Clicking the Inbox link opens your text messages for reading. Alternatively, you can click the **SMS** link to see just your text messages.

3. Find the text message you want to report as spam and check the check box beside it.

4. Click the **Report as Spam** button. Google Voice funnels further messages from this sender straight into the Spam inbox.

Sometimes a message may be marked as spam in error. You can change your mind and remove the spam label from a sender. Here's how:

1. Navigate to the Google Voice site and log in (if necessary).

2. On the left side of the page, click **Spam**. This opens an inbox that contains all the messages you've received that have been marked as spam.

3. Find the text message that's not actually spam and check the check box beside it.

4. Click the **Not Spam** button. Google Voice removes the Spam label and moves the message into your Inbox.

Summary

As you learned in this Lesson, text messaging with Google Voice is both easy and flexible. Lesson 8, "Going Mobile," frees you from your computer, showing how to use and manage Google Voice from your mobile phone.

LESSON 8

Going Mobile

Mobile phones are everywhere, and Google Voice fully supports them. This lesson explains the special concerns of using Google Voice with mobile phones.

Getting Calls on a Mobile Phone

As you saw in Lesson 2, "Signing Up and Getting Started," when you set up Google Voice, you designate the phones you'll be using. There are two choices when you sign up:

▶ Get a new Google Voice number

▶ Use an existing number

If you set up Google Voice to use an existing number, that number must be a mobile phone number—and that mobile phone is the only phone you can use with your Google Voice account. Using an existing mobile phone number to sign up for Google Voice means that you'll use only that mobile phone with Google Voice for voicemail, contacts, and so on.

Your friends and contacts still call your existing mobile phone number, but Google Voice handles voicemail and so forth. Google Voice does give a new number, but that's for your exclusive use for picking up your voice-mails and for making calls through Google Voice.

Although it's possible to retain your mobile phone number to use with Google Voice, most people simply add their mobile phone as a forwarding phone in their multiple-phone Google Voice account. That way, calls come in on your mobile phone, as well as your other forwarding phones. The next section shows you how to forward calls from your Google Voice number to your mobile phone.

Forwarding to Mobile Phones

You can set up call forwarding to mobile phones easily—just follow these steps:

1. Navigate to the Google Voice site and log in (if necessary).

2. Click the **Settings** link to open the Settings page.

3. Click the **Phones** tab, as shown in Figure 8.1. The Phones tab displays your Google Voice number. Beneath it, you see a list of the phones you've registered with Google Voice.

FIGURE 8.1   The Phones tab of the Settings page.

4. Place a check mark next to any phones you want to ring when someone calls your Google Voice number. Checking the phones you want Google Voice to ring makes Google Voice call those phones when someone calls your Google Voice number.

5. Click the left-hand **Inbox** link. This takes you back to the Google Voice home page.

You can add new mobile phones to the list of phones Google Voice knows about as well. Just follow these steps:

1. Navigate to the Google Voice site and log in (if necessary).

2. Click the **Settings** link to open the Settings page.

3. Click the **Phones** tab. The Phones tab opens, displaying the phones currently connected to your Google Voice number.

4. Click the **Add Another Phone** link. Doing so opens the page you see in Figure 8.2.

FIGURE 8.2   Adding a new phone.

5. Enter a name for the new phone. Give your new phone a name, such as "My Mobile."

6. Enter the number of the new phone.

7. Select the type of phone you're adding. Select the Mobile option to add a new mobile phone to the list.

8. Check the **Receive SMS on This Phone** checkbox if you wish to use SMS text messaging with this phone.

9. If you want to set voicemail access (Lesson 3, "Making a Call") or a ring schedule (Lesson 4, "Answering a Call"), click the **Show Advanced Settings** link.

10. Click the **Save** button to save the new phone. A dialog box appears that tells you that Google Voice needs to confirm the new phone and displays a two-digit verification code.

11. Click the **Connect** button in the dialog box. Google Voice calls you on the new phone.

12. Pick up the phone. Google Voice asks you to enter your verification code.

13. Enter the verification code on the phone. Google Voice confirms your new phone and hangs up.

And that's it—now you've added a new mobile phone to your Google Voice account. You can now set up this phone to receive forwarded calls.

Forwarding a Group to a Mobile Phone

Many people use their mobile phones primarily to receive calls from a specific group, such as their coworkers or family. When you've added contacts to a group (see Lesson 6, "Working with Contacts and Groups"), you can forward calls made to you by members of that group to your mobile phone. Here's how:

1. Navigate to the Google Voice site and log in (if necessary).

2. Click the **Settings** link to open the Settings page.

3. Click **Groups**. Clicking the Groups tab displays all your groups in a list.

4. Click the **Edit** button for the group whose settings you want to change. This opens the settings for the particular group you're interested in, as you can see in Figure 8.3.

5. In the When People in This Group Call You section, click the **Edit** link. Clicking this link displays the list of forwarding phones that you've set up with Google Voice.

6. Put a check mark next to the mobile phone you want to forward calls from the group to.

7. Click the **Save** button. Google Voice saves your new setting.

Now when people from that group call you, their calls will ring the mobile phone you've indicated.

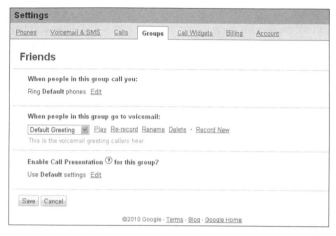

FIGURE 8.3   Editing a group's settings.

Setting Up Temporary Forwarding

Sometimes when you're away from the office, such as on a business trip, you might want to set up temporary call forwarding to your mobile phone. That's a great use of Google Voice—sending your calls to your mobile phone until you get back to the office. Here's how to do it:

1. Call your Google number from your mobile phone.

2. Press * and enter your PIN if you're calling from a phone you haven't set up for forwarding with Google Voice. If you're calling from a phone for which you've already set up for forwarding, just enter your PIN (no * required).

3. Press **4** to access the Settings menu.

4. Press **4** again to access your temporary settings.

5. Press **2** to set up a temporary forwarding number.

6. Press # to add the number you're calling from or **1** followed by a number and then followed by # to add a different number.

To turn off temporary call forwarding, follow these steps:

1. Call your Google number.

2. Press * and enter your PIN if you're calling from a phone you haven't set up for forwarding with Google Voice. If you're calling from a phone for which you've already set up for forwarding, just enter your PIN (no * required).

3. Press **4** to access the Settings menu.

4. Press **4** again to access your temporary settings.

5. Press **2** to set up a temporary forwarding number.

6. Press **3** to turn off your temporary forwarding number.

Getting Voicemail Notification with SMS

Google Voice will text your mobile phone when you receive a voicemail. Here's how to set that up:

1. Navigate to the Google Voice site and log in (if necessary).

2. Click the **Settings** link to open the Settings page.

3. Click the **Voicemail & SMS** tab. The tab you see in Figure 8.4 opens.

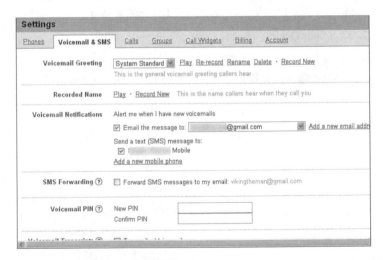

FIGURE 8.4   The Voicemail & SMS tab.

4. In the Voicemail Notifications section, check the checkbox next to the mobile phone(s) that you want to receive the voicemail notification text message.

5. Click the **Save Changes** button. Google Voice saves the new setting.

Now Google Voice will alert you with a text message to this phone whenever you get a new voicemail.

Turning Off Calls

There are situations when you may not want to receive calls on your mobile phone—when you're in a meeting or at the movies, for example. In such situations, you can simply turn off or silence your phone. Or you can use Google Voice's Do Not Disturb setting.

This setting turns off all calls for a while, sending everyone to voicemail—that way, your mobile phone won't ring while you're in the meeting. You can turn off all calls temporarily this way:

1. Navigate to the Google Voice site and log in (if necessary).

2. Click the **Settings** link to open the Settings page.

3. Click the **Calls** tab. This displays the tab where you'll find the Do Not Disturb setting, as shown in Figure 8.5.

4. In the Do Not Disturb section, check the **Enable "Do Not Disturb"** checkbox. This turns on the Do Not Disturb setting.

5. Click the **Save Changes** button. Google Voice applies the Do Not Disturb setting to all of your phones.

All calls are sent to voicemail while you have Do Not Disturb enabled. To get your phones ringing again, follow the same steps, but uncheck the Enable "Do Not Disturb" checkbox in step 4.

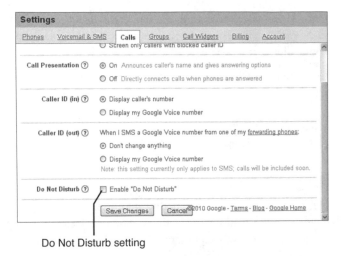

Do Not Disturb setting

FIGURE 8.5   Enabling the Do Not Disturb setting.

Making Calls from a Mobile Phone

If you have a mobile phone, even one you've connected to a multiple-phone Google Voice account, there's nothing stopping you from making calls directly from that mobile phone—and those calls won't involve Google Voice. In other words, you can still use your mobile phone as usual to make calls.

But what if you want people to start using your Google Voice number? In that case, it makes sense to go through Google Voice when you make a call from your mobile phone. That way, your Google Voice number will be the number people will call back.

> NOTE
>
> If you signed up for Google Voice using your existing mobile phone number, the mobile phone number always appears as the number you're calling from. That's true even when you call through Google Voice.

One excellent reason to make a call through Google Voice from your mobile phone is when you call internationally. Usually, Google Voice won't save you money on domestic mobile phone calls, because your mobile phone carrier still charges you for the minutes you use. Some carriers, like AT&T, let you call other subscribers on the same network for free—but that won't work if you're calling through Google Voice, because the Google Voice number makes your phone look like it's not a subscriber on the same network.

But international calls are often very expensive with most U.S. mobile phone carriers—and those same calls are very cheap with Google Voice. So when you make an international call, you end up paying just pennies more than you'd pay for a domestic call of the same length. If you make international calls, you can save a lot of money using Google Voice to make them. Lesson 9, "Billing and International Calls," tells you all about making international calls with Google Voice.

> TIP
>
> The ability to make cheap international calls also appears to be a good reason for some carriers to block Google Voice. For example, the iPhone doesn't support applications that were originally introduced to let you use Google Voice on your iPhone.

Using Android Phones

Google developed the Android operating system, so you might expect that Android-enabled phones can make good use of Google Voice—and you'd be right.

You can use Google Voice with the default dialer app that's built into Android. (That's not the case on the BlackBerry or the iPhone.) Here's a list of advantages of using Google Voice with phones running Android:

- ▶ **Easy voicemail integration.** Voicemail transcripts are displayed directly in Android phones, so there's no need to go to the Google Voice mobile site.

- ▶ **Call history is kept updated.** You can access your Google Voice call history as part of the Android operating system.

▶ **Google Voice can handle your voicemail.** There's no need to use the phone's default voicemail system. You get all the features and flexibility of Google Voice voicemail instead. (Lesson 5, "Using Voicemail," tells you all about those.)

▶ **Google Voice is in the default dialer.** As mentioned, unlike on the BlackBerry or iPhone, Google Voice is built right into the default dialer in Android phones.

▶ **Integrated notifications.** Unlike on some other phones, you're notified when you get a voicemail or SMS even if a Google Voice app isn't running.

▶ **You don't need to make an intermediate phone call.** Google Voice connects you using the same call.

▶ **You don't have to log in.** Android stores your Google Voice log-in and signs in for you.

▶ **SMS is free.** And free is always a good thing.

▶ **You can use your Contacts.** The contacts you store on an Android phone can be contacted directly via Google Voice.

Using BlackBerry Phones

Google Voice has an app that runs on BlackBerry phones. Although the integration of that app with Google Voice isn't as good as with Android phones, you can still enjoy these advantages:

▶ **SMS is free.** If you send and receive a lot of text messages, free SMS is a big advantage.

▶ **Integrated notifications.** You don't need to have the Google Voice app running to receive notifications when someone calls or texts you.

▶ **You can use your contacts.** You can call the contacts you've stored on your BlackBerry phone directly through Google Voice.

Unlike using an Android phone, you need to make an intermediate call to use Google Voice via your BlackBerry. You call the special number Google Voice has given you, and Google Voice calls you back.

Using iPhones

The Apple iPhone us the most popular smart phone in history—so why does it come last in our list of mobile phones, after Android phones and the BlackBerry?

It's because the iPhone is down on Google Voice. The iPhone App Store no longer lists the apps that, in the past, you could use to access Google Voice on the iPhone. Technically speaking, the iPhone frowns on Google Voice.

It's not clear whether that's due to the cheap international calling you can do through Google Voice or to some other reason. But one thing's for sure—the iPhone App Store doesn't carry any Google Voice dialers, which let you integrate Google Voice with the iPhone.

If you want to use Google Voice with your iPhone, though, don't despair. You can still call Google Voice yourself from an iPhone. In fact, take a look at the next section. It tells you how to make it easier to use Google Voice on phones that aren't Google Voice friendly.

Faking Google Voice Dialers

If your phone doesn't integrate easily with Google Voice—that is, if you can't use a dialer to call Google Voice automatically—all may not be lost. If your phone lets you store long numbers for your contacts, you might be able to convince your phone to dial Google Voice automatically by using a workaround.

Here's how it works: In one contact, you store *all* of the digits you need to dial Google Voice, pass the number you're calling to Google Voice, and also the number you want to be called back on. If you can store all that for a single contact, then using Google Voice is easy—just ask your phone to dial that contact.

For each contact you want to dial through Google Voice, follow these steps:

1. Start with your Google Voice number. If your Google Voice number is *xxxxxxxxxx*, enter that as the number to call for this contact. (Replace all those *x*'s with your actual Google Voice number.)

2. Enter the pause key for your phone. The pause key is usually a comma, so the number for the contact so far is $xxxxxxxxxx,$. (No period at the end.)

3. If you use a PIN, enter an asterisk (*). This tells Google Voice to get ready to accept your PIN. Now, the number for the contact so far is $xxxxxxxxxx,*$. (No period at the end.)

4. If you use a PIN, enter the pause key for your phone. The pause key is usually a comma, so at this point, the number for the contact is $xxxxxxxxxx,*,$. (No period at the end.)

5. If you use a PIN, enter it now. If your PIN is $yyyy$, the number so far becomes $xxxxxxxxxx,*,yyyy$. (No period at the end, and the y's are replaced by your actual PIN.)

6. If you use a PIN, enter the pause key for your phone. The pause key is usually a comma, so the number for the contact so far is $xxxxxxxxxx,*,yyyy,$. (No period at the end.)

7. Enter a 2 to tell Google Voice that you want to make a call. That makes the number for this contact so far $xxxxxxxxxx,*,yyyy,2$. (No period at the end.)

8. Enter the pause key for your phone. The pause key is usually a comma, making the number for the contact so far $xxxxxxxxxx,*,yyyy,2,$. (No period at the end.)

9. Enter the contact's phone number. If your contact's number is $zzzzzzzzzz$, that would make the number so far $xxxxxxxxxx,*,yyyy,2,zzzzzzzzzz$. (No period at the end, and replace those 10 z's with the actual phone number.)

10. Enter a pound sign (#)to tell Google Voice you're done entering the number. So the final number you're storing is $xxxxxxxxxx,*,yyyy,2,zzzzzzzzzz#$. (No period at the end.)

So to store a contact, you enter $xxxxxxxxxx,*,yyyy,2,zzzzzzzzzz#$ where:

▶ $xxxxxxxxxx$ is your 10-digit Google Voice number.

▶ $yyyy$ is your PIN (if you use one).

▶ $zzzzzzzzzz$ is the 10-digit phone number of your contact.

This method won't work on all mobile phones, because some can't store numbers that long. But if you don't have easy access to Google Voice through your mobile phone, it's worth a try.

Using the Google Voice Mobile Site

The Google Voice mobile site is designed to be used from any mobile phone that has a web browser. If Google Voice isn't integrated into your phone, the mobile site is your entry point for using Google Voice.

You'll find the Google Voice mobile site at www.google.com/voice/m. Figure 8.6 shows you what the site looks like.

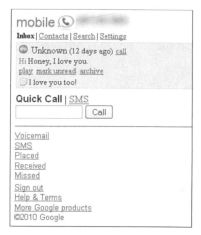

FIGURE 8.6   The Google Voice mobile site.

The Google Voice mobile site gives you mobile phone access to everything that the regular Google Voice website offers. And here's good news for iPhone users: You can use the mobile site with your iPhone. In other words, you don't need a Google Voice app to use Google Voice with your iPhone.

We'll explore the Google Voice mobile site now, starting by making a call.

Making a Call

To use the Google Voice mobile site to place a call, just follow these steps:

1. Navigate to the Google Voice mobile site and log in (if necessary). The Google Voice mobile site appears in your phone's browser.

2. In the Quick Call box, enter the number you want to call.

3. Click the **Call** button. Google Voice calls your mobile number. Then, it calls the number you're calling and connects you.

If have several phones registered with Google Voice, you need to let Google Voice know which one to use when you're placing a call. To tell Google Voice which mobile phone to call you back on, do this:

1. Navigate to the Google Voice mobile site and log in (if necessary). The Google Voice mobile site appears in your phone's browser.

2. Click the **Settings** link to open the Settings page, as you see in Figure 8.7.

3. Click the **My Mobile Number** link. Clicking this link displays your registered Google Voice phone numbers, as shown in Figure 8.8.

4. Find the phone you want and click its radio button. This tells Google Voice to connect you using this phone number when you make a call.

5. Click the **Save** button. Google Voice saves the phone number you chose.

FIGURE 8.7   The Google Voice mobile site's Settings page.

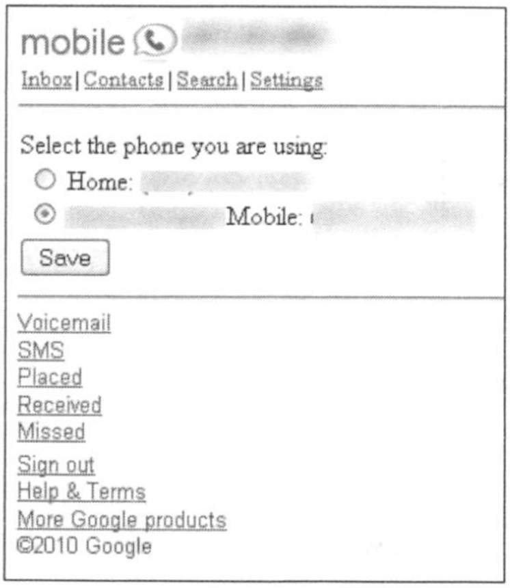

FIGURE 8.8   Setting your current mobile phone.

Sending a Text Message

Google Voice lets you send text messages for free, and that gives it a definite edge over carriers that charge you for text messages. To send a text message from the Google Voice mobile site, do this:

1. Navigate to the Google Voice mobile site and log in (if necessary). The Google Voice mobile site appears in your phone's browser.

2. Click the **SMS** link in the Quick Call section. This opens the page you see in Figure 8.9.

FIGURE 8.9   Sending a text message through the mobile site.

3. In the To box, enter the recipient's number.

4. Type your message in the Message box.

5. Click the **Send** button.

Your text message is on its way.

Receiving Voicemail

The Google Voice mobile site lets you pick up your voicemail, just as the full Google Voice site does. To check your voicemail on the mobile site, follow these steps:

1. Navigate to the Google Voice mobile site and log in (if necessary).

2. Click the **Inbox** link to open the Inbox, as you see in Figure 8.10.

   Your voicemail messages are displayed in the Inbox, just as they are on the full Google Voice website. Each voicemail and SMS message is transcribed and displayed.

FIGURE 8.10   The mobile site's Inbox.

3. Click the **Play** link.

4. To return the call, click the message's **Call** link.

Using Contacts

The Google Voice mobile site gives you easy access to the contacts you've set up in your Google Voice account. To access any contact, follow these quick steps:

1. Navigate to the Google Voice mobile site and log in (if necessary). The Google Voice mobile site appears in your phone's browser.

2. Click the **Contacts** link. This opens the page you see in Figure 8.11.

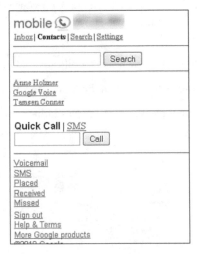

FIGURE 8.11   Your contacts on the mobile site.

3. Click the name of the contact you want to call. Doing so opens a page for the contact, like the one you see in Figure 8.12.

4. To call the contact, click the **Call** button.

5. To text the contact, click the **SMS** button.

FIGURE 8.12   A contact's page on the mobile site.

Turning Off Calls from Your Mobile Phone

Earlier in this lesson, you read about the Do Not Disturb setting, which prevents your phone from ringing and sends calls straight to voicemail—a useful setting when you're busy, in a meeting, or just want a little peace and quiet. You can turn on the Do Not Disturb setting directly from your mobile phone.

Here's how to turn on the Do Not Disturb setting from your mobile phone:

1. Navigate to the Google Voice mobile site and log in (if necessary). The Google Voice mobile site appears in your phone's browser.

2. Click the **Settings** link.

3. Click the **Do Not Disturb** link. This opens the page you see in Figure 8.13.

FIGURE 8.13   The Do Not Disturb page on the Google Voice mobile site.

4. Check the **Enable "Do Not Disturb"** checkbox.

5. Click the **Save** button. Google Voice applies the Do Not Disturb setting to your phone.

Now Google Voice won't interrupt you with a ringing phone when a call comes in. To turn off Do Not Disturb (and start getting calls on this phone again), repeat the same steps, unchecking the Enable "Do Not Disturb" checkbox in step 4.

Introducing the Google Voice Web App

At this writing, Google Voice is coming up with a way to circumvent the iPhone's restrictions on Google Voice apps: Google Voice Web apps, which you access through HTML 5-enabled browsers in smart phones. And that includes the iPhone.

To access the Google Voice Web app, just use your phone's browser to go to the main Google Voice mobile site. (For the iPhone, that's Safari.) Although the Google Voice Web app is still under development at this point, you'll be able to use it to dial your Google Voice contacts directly, even on an iPhone.

Summary

This Lesson showed you how to use Google Voice from your mobile phone. In Lesson 9 you'll learn how to save money by making inexpensive international calls.

LESSON 9

Billing and International Calls

Many people choose Google Voice for one very good reason: inexpensive international calling. Calls inside the U.S. and Canada are free with Google Voice, but international calls to locations other than Canada will cost you.

If you've ever made international calls using a mobile phone, you know that calling another country can cost several dollars per minute. Even overseas calling from landlines can be unreasonably expensive. But Google Voice is different; it represents just about the best rates you'll find for international calls from the U.S. (other than using your parents' phone for free). The cheap rates aren't available when you make international calls through Google Voice from countries outside the U.S. and Canada.

> **NOTE**
>
> Many commentators have theorized that it's cheap international calling—plus free text messages—that have irked AT&T enough to get Google Voice apps bounced from the iPhone.

Whenever money is involved, there's the possibility of mistakes, so we also talk about how to get your money back from Google Voice and how to make sure your transactions are secure.

All this is coming up in this chapter, starting with international calling.

Making International Calls

Using Google Voice, you can call internationally using either the website or your phone—we take a look at both ways here.

> TIP
>
> Considering international calls cost money, later in this lesson we take a look at how to add money to your Google Voice account.

Determining International Calling Rates

How much can you save when you use Google Voice to make international calls? That depends on where you call, of course, your phone company's current rates, and a few other factors. A quick check shows that calls to Afghanistan currently run $0.27 per minute through Google Voice. My personal landline is a digital phone through the cable company with unlimited U.S. calling—but calling Afghanistan would cost $1.07 per minute. And a popular mobile phone plan charges up to $2.99 per minute to call that country. So in this example, the Google Voice savings are significant.

You can check international rates easily by taking these steps:

1. Navigate to the Google Voice site and log in if necessary.

2. Click the **Settings** link to open the Settings page.

3. Click the **Billing** tab. The Billing tab opens, as shown in Figure 9.1.

FIGURE 9.1   The Billing tab of the settings page.

4. Click the **See Rates** link. Clicking this link opens the page shown in Figure 9.2.

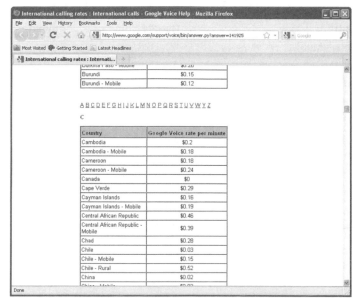

FIGURE 9.2 Google Voice international calling rates.

There are many pages of international calling rates available—Table 9.1 shows you a sample.

TABLE 9.1 A Sample of Google Voice International Rates

Country	Google Voice rate per minute
Afghanistan	$0.27
Albania	$0.12
Albania—Mobile	$0.25
Albania—Tirane	$0.12
Algeria	$0.12
Algeria—Mobile	$0.26
Algeria—Mobile—Orascom	$0.37
Algeria—Mobile—Wataniya	$0.37
American Samoa	$0.07
Andorra	$0.04
Andorra—Mobile	$0.22
Angola	$0.14

TABLE 9.1 Continued

Country	Google Voice rate per minute
Angola—Mobile	$0.18
Anguilla	$0.12
Anguilla—Mobile	$0.24
Antarctica	$2.00
Antigua and Barbuda	$0.14
Argentina	$0.02
Argentina—Buenos Aires	$0.02
Argentina—Buenos Aires—Mobile	$0.01
Argentina—Mobile	$0.12
Armenia	$0.09
Armenia—Mobile	$0.21
Aruba	$0.12
Aruba—Mobile	$0.23
Ascension Island	$1.90
Australia	$0.02
Australia—Mobile	$0.14
Australia—Satellite Services	$0.17
Austria	$0.03
Austria—Mobile	$0.19
Austria—Premium	$0.45
Azerbaijan	$0.17
Azerbaijan—Mobile	$0.24

Note that the rates shown are as of this writing and will most likely change.

Calling from the Website

As you'd expect, you can make international calls from the Google Voice website. When you do, Google Voice calls you on the phone you specify and then connects your international call.

Here's how to make an international call from the Google Voice website:

   1. Navigate to the Google Voice site and log in if necessary.

2. Click the **Call** button. Clicking the Call button opens a drop-down window, as shown in Figure 9.3.

FIGURE 9.3 The Call button's drop-down window.

3. In the Call box, enter the number you want to call. For international calls, enter "+*country code*" or "+1*countrycode*" (depending on where you're calling) followed by the international number.

For example: +442012345612345 or +1246-426-1234.

4. Select the phone you want to use for the call. Google Voice lists the phones you've registered. Select the phone you want to use for this call. This is the phone Google Voice calls you on before it connects you to the international number.

> TIP
>
> If you want Google Voice always to call you on the phone you've just selected, check the **Remember My Choice** check box. (You can select a different phone whenever you want.)

5. Click **Connect**. Google Voice calls you on the phone you've selected. When you pick it up, you'll hear the other phone ringing. When the person you're calling answers, the call is completed.

6. In the drop-down Call window, click the upper-right X button to close that window. The drop-down window that appeared when you clicked the Call button stays open even when your call is complete. To close it, click its upper-right X button.

That's all there is to it—you're talking to your overseas contact (and for just pennies a minute).

You can add new phones to the list that Google Voice will call back. Just follow these steps:

1. Navigate to the Google Voice site and log in if necessary.

2. Click the **Settings** link to open the Settings page.

3. Click the **Phones** tab. The Phones tab opens, displaying the phones currently connected to your Google Voice number.

4. Click the Add Another Phone link.

5. Enter a name for the new phone. Choose a name that helps you identify which phone this is, such as "My Mobile."

6. Enter the phone number.

7. Select the type of phone you're adding. These are your choices:

   ▶ Mobile

   ▶ Work

   ▶ Home

   ▶ Other

8. If you wish to use SMS text messaging with this phone, check the **Receive SMS on This Phone (mobile phones only)** checkbox.

TIP

The Show Advanced Settings link lets you set Voicemail access (covered in Lesson 3, "Making a Call,") and a ring schedule (covered in Lesson 4, "Answering a Call").

---

9. Click the **Save** button to save the new phone. Google Voice shows a dialog box that tells you it needs to confirm the new phone and displays a two-digit verification code.

10. Click the **Connect** button in the dialog box. Google Voice calls you on the new phone.

11. Pick up the phone. Google Voice asks you to enter your verification code.

12. Enter the verification code on the phone. Google Voice confirms your new phone and hangs up.

Now you can use this phone to make international calls through Google Voice.

Calling from Your Phone

You can also use Google Voice to make international calls directly from your phone, whether it's a mobile phone or a landline.

Here's how:

1. Dial your Google Voice number. Just pick up any phone and dial your Google Voice number.

2. During the greeting press *. The system prompts you to enter your PIN—not with a voice prompt, but with a simple beep.

3. Enter your PIN.

4. From the list of options Google Voice gives you, select option **2**. When you press 2, you'll be prompted to enter the number you want to call.

5. Enter the number you want to call. For international calls, dial 011, the country code, then the number (for example: 011442012345612345).

6. Press #. (Pressing # tells Google Voice that you've finished entering the number.) Google Voice then connects you to the number you entered.

As you can see, calling directly from your phone is quick and easy—and very handy when you're not online to use the Google Voice website.

Of course, you can also use your phone's web browser to place an international call. To make an overseas call from the mobile site, follow these steps:

1. Navigate to the Google Voice mobile site at www.google.com/voice/m. Figure 9.4 shows you what this site looks like.

FIGURE 9.4   The Google Voice mobile website.

2. Click the **Call** button. A drop-down window opens.

3. In the **Quick Call** box, enter the number you want to call. For international calls, dial 011, the country code, and then the number.

4. Select the phone you want to use for the call. Google Voice lists the phones you've registered. Select the phone you want to use for this call. This is the phone Google Voice calls you on before it connects you to the international number.

NOTE

Google Voice will remember the phone you asked to be called on. The next time you make a call from the Google Voice mobile page, Google Voice will automatically select that phone.

---

5. Click **Call**. Google Voice calls you on the phone you've selected. When you pick it up, you'll hear the other phone ringing. When the person you're calling answers, the call is completed.

As you've seen, calling through your phone's browser is quick and easy.

You've seen the different ways to place an international call through Google Voice. Now let's see about how to pay for your international calls.

Billing

They say talk is cheap. When you use Google Voice, that's true even for international calls. But you've still got to pay for those cheap calls. The rest of this chapter deals with billing issues and how to pay Google Voice for calling minutes you can use to make international calls.

Google Voice takes money through Google Checkout, and if you haven't used Google Checkout before, it's pretty easy. Let's start by adding some money to an account and then begin paying for those international calls.

Adding Money to Your Account

When you open a Google Voice account, you start off with ten cents in the account (as you can see Figure 9.5). Even with inexpensive overseas rates, that won't buy you much talk time. You can add money to your Google Voice account in $10 increments—here's how:

1. Navigate to the Google Voice site and log in if necessary.

2. Click the **Settings** link to open the Settings page.

3. Click the **Billing** tab. The Billing tab opens, as shown in Figure 9.5.

4. Click the **Add Credit** link. A drop-down box appears with one option, $10—that's your only choice.

FIGURE 9.5 The Billing tab of the Settings page.

5. Click the **$10** item. Google Checkout opens, as shown in Figures 9.6 and 9.7.

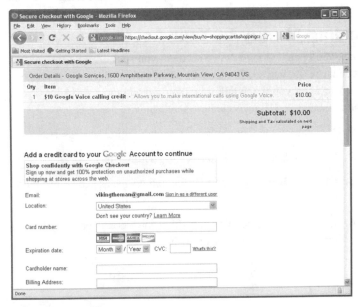

FIGURE 9.6 The Google Checkout page, top half.

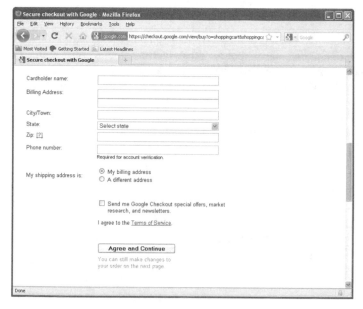

FIGURE 9.7 The Google Checkout page, bottom half.

Your email address (the one you use for your Google account) already appears on the Google Accounts page.

6. Select your country from the drop-down Country box. The United States is selected by default.

7. Enter the information requested on the form.

> NOTE
>
> You might wonder why Google Checkout requires your phone number for a simple credit card purchase. Google Checkout says it needs your phone number for card verification, and it won't process the transaction until you enter it.

8. In the "My shipping address is" section, select the **My Billing Address** radio button if your shipping address is the same as the billing address. If you want to use a different address for shipping, select the **A Different Address** radio button, which causes text boxes to appear for you to enter your shipping address.

> NOTE
>
> Why do you need to bother with a shipping address? After all, when you purchase calling credits, nothing gets "shipped" anywhere. The advantage is when you use Google Checkout for other purchases. If your shipping address is different from your billing address for actual physical shipments, you can enter them both here. In the future, Google Checkout will remember both of these addresses for other items you buy that do require shipping.

9. Check the **Send Me Google Checkout Special Offers, Market Research, and Newsletters** checkbox if you want to receive all kinds of email from Google Checkout. Some people like getting these special offers; others consider them spam. If you don't want Google emailing you with such stuff, leave this box unchecked.

10. Click the **Agree and Continue** button. Clicking this button opens the login page for your Google Account, as shown in Figure 9.8.

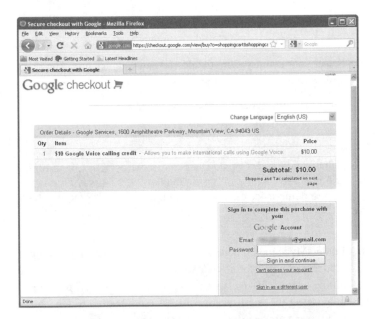

FIGURE 9.8   The Google Accounts sign-in page, bottom half.

11. Enter the same password you use to log in to Google Voice.

12. Click the **Sign in and Continue** button. Clicking this button opens the page you see in Figure 9.9.

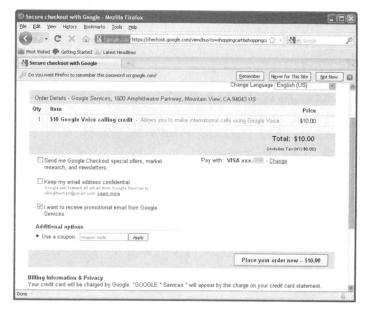

FIGURE 9.9 Purchasing phone credits.

13. Check the **Send Me Google Checkout Special Offers, Market Research, and Newsletters** checkbox if you want to receive all kinds of email from Google Checkout. If you don't want Google emailing you with such stuff, leave this box unchecked.

14. Check the **Keep My Email Address Confidential** checkbox if you don't want your email to show on your purchases.

15. Check the **I Want to Receive Promotional Email from Google Services** checkbox if you want such email from Google Services. Again, some people consider promotional email spam. If that's you, leave the box unchecked.

16. If you have a Google Checkout coupon, enter its code in the **Use a Coupon** box and click the **Apply** button. Otherwise, leave this box blank.

17. Click the **Place Your Order Now** button. Clicking this button opens the page you see in Figure 9.10.

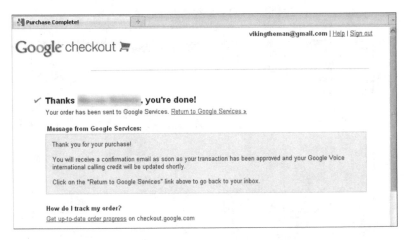

FIGURE 9.10   Confirming a purchase.

18. When you've finished adding money to your Google Voice account, click the **Return to Google Services** link. This returns you to your Inbox in Google Voice.

Congratulations! It took several steps, but you've added $10 to your Google Voice account. Now you can use it to make international calls.

Before you make an international call, it's good to know how much money you've got in your account. So now that you've added some money, let's check the balance.

Checking Your Google Voice Account Balance

You can check your remaining balance at any time on the Google Voice website. Here's how to do that:

1. Navigate to the Google Voice site and log in if necessary.

2. Click the **Settings** link to open the Settings page.

3. Click the **Billing** tab. The Billing tab opens, as shown in Figure 9.11. At the top of this tab, you can see your current balance ($10.10 in the figure).

FIGURE 9.11 The Billing tab shows your current balance.

> NOTE
>
> The Billing tab also lists a history of your credit purchases. Whenever you want, you can check to see where your money has gone.

If you find you're not using your credit, is there some way to get your money back? Yes, and that's coming up next.

Refunding Your Google Voice Credit Purchase

If you've deposited more money in your Google Voice account than you're using to make calls, you can get your money back. If you want a refund from Google, you can get it this way:

1. Locate the order receipt you received. When you purchased Google Voice credit, the receipt was sent to the email address associated with your Google account.

2. In your email program, open the message containing the receipt.

3. In the email message, find the "Problems with order?" section and click the **Contact Google Apps** link. This opens a web page in your browser.

4. In the web page that opens, click the **Subject** drop-down menu and select **I'd Like to Request a Refund or Return an Item**.

5. In the Message field, enter the reason you're requesting a refund.

6. Click the **Send** button. This submits your refund request to Google Checkout.

Google reviews your request and lets you know the result.

Sometimes, you don't want a refund for the credits you purchased—you just want a refund for the call. This might happen, for example, when you accidentally dial the wrong number. To request a refund for a particular call, follow these steps:

1. Navigate to the Google Voice site and log in if necessary. This makes sure you are logged in.

2. Navigate to https://www.google.com/voice/billing/credits. This page lists your most recent international calls that are eligible for refunds.

> NOTE
>
> Note that Google Voice lists only short calls as eligible for a refund. If you stayed on the phone for a longer call, Google Voice assumes that the call was OK.

3. Select the call(s) you want to get a refund for. Place a check in the checkbox next to all such calls.

4. Click the **Request Refund** button. Your request is submitted to Google.

Later, you get an email letting you know whether or not you will be receiving a refund.

Changing Your Payment Information

You can change your shipping address or credit card information at any time with Google Checkout. Here's how to change your default shipping address:

1. Navigate to the Google Checkout at https://checkout.google.com and log in. The Google Checkout site displays a web page showing your recent purchases.

2. Click the **Edit Shipping Addresses** link. Clicking this link displays a page that shows the shipping address Google Checkout has for you.

3. Select the country of the new shipping address from the drop-down Location list. The default is the United States.

4. Enter the information requested on the form.

5. If this is the shipping address you always want to use from now on, check the checkbox labeled Make This My Default Shipping Address.

6. Click the **Save** button. Google Checkout saves your changes.

You've successfully entered a new shipping address in Google Checkout.

To change or update your credit card information, follow these steps:

1. Navigate to the Google Checkout at https://checkout.google.com and log in. The Google Checkout site displays a web page showing your recent purchases.

2. Click the **Edit Payment Methods** link. Clicking this link displays a page that lets you change your credit card information.

3. Select the country of the new credit card from the drop-down Location list. The default is the United States.

4. Enter the information requested on the form.

> NOTE
>
> Google Checkout requires a phone number for credit card verification.

5. If you want this credit card to become the default in your Google Checkout account, check the checkbox labeled **Make This My Default Payment Method**.

6. Click the **Save** button. Google Checkout saves your new credit card information.

The credit card you entered is now associated with your Google Voice account, and you can use it to make future purchases.

Reporting Abuse

Whenever money and the Internet come together, there's a potential for abuse. Someone may use your Google Checkout account without your authorization, for example, or you may see charges you don't recognize.

If you suspect someone is abusing your Google Checkout account, you should report the abuse as soon as you spot it. Here's how:

1. Navigate to https://checkout.google.com/support/bin/request.py? contact_type=ua. This gets you to the Google Checkout abuse page, as shown in Figure 9.12.

2. Enter the information requested on the form.

3. Choose the kind of abuse you're reporting:

   ▶ My Google Checkout account was accessed without my authorization.

   ▶ My billing statement includes an unrecognized charge from Google.

4. Click the **Submit** button. Your problem is reported to Google.

Google reviews your abuse report and gets back to you.

You can also contact Google Checkout about security concerns this way:

1. Navigate to https://checkout.google.com/support/bin/request.py.

2. Click the **Security & Privacy** radio button.

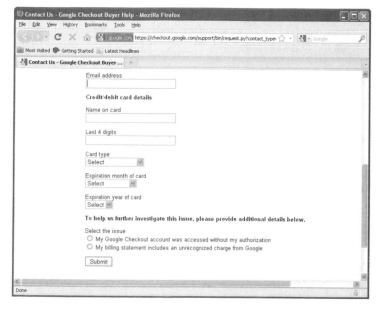

FIGURE 9.12   The Google Checkout abuse page.

3. Click the radio button that describes your problem:

   ▶ Account access

   ▶ Unauthorized charges

4. For issues related to account access, click one of these three radio buttons:

   ▶ Forgot my password.

   ▶ Forgot my username.

   ▶ I think someone took over my account.

5. For issues related to unauthorized charges, click one of these three radio buttons:

   ▶ Charged twice for same order.

   ▶ Charged an extra $1.

   ▶ Never made a purchase.

6. Click the **Continue** button. Google Checkout takes you to a page that asks for more specific details about your problem. Fill out the required information.

7. Click the **Submit** button. This reports your issue to Google Voice.

You've now let Google Voice know about the problem you're having. How Google responds depends on the specific issue you've reported.

Summary

Now you can make international calls for a lot less money using Google Voice. Lesson 10, "Troubleshooting Google Voice," makes you a true Google Voice expert by showing you how to work around common issues and problems you might encounter.

LESSON 10

Troubleshooting Google Voice

As you might expect with a system as complex as Google Voice, plenty of things can go wrong—and this lesson gives you the information and tools to help you fix those problems.

We tackle all kinds of issues in this lesson, from making it easier for people to call you to debugging what's happening when SMS messages go missing.

Making It Easier for Others to Call You

If people have trouble remembering your Google Voice phone number, you can make it easier for them with a call widget. A call widget is a button that you embed in a web page; people can simply click the button to call you.

When someone clicks the call widget, Google Voice asks the caller to enter his or her phone number. Google Voice calls that number, calls you, and then connects the calls. Presto! You're talking to the caller who used the widget.

Here's how to create your own call widget:

1. Navigate to the Google Voice site and log in if necessary.

2. Click the **Settings** link to open the Settings page.

3. Click the **Call Widgets** tab.

4. Click the **Add a New Call Widget** link. A new page appears, as shown in Figures 10.1 and 10.2. You can see what the call widget will look like in your web page in Figure 10.1.

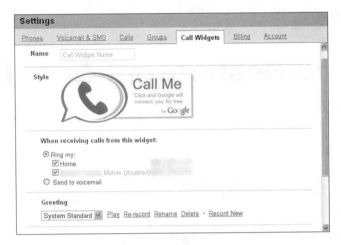

FIGURE 10.1 The Call Widgets tab of the Settings page, top half.

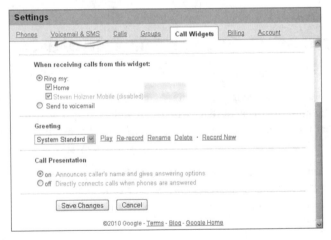

FIGURE 10.2 The Call Widgets tab of the Settings page, bottom half.

5. Enter a name for the call widget in the Name box. If you create more than one widget, giving each one a name helps you tell them apart.

6. In the When Receiving Calls from This Widget: section, select the **Ring My** or the **Voicemail** radio button. If you selected the Ring My radio button, use the checkboxes under the radio button

to select the phone(s) you want to ring when someone uses the call widget.

7. Select a greeting in the Greeting section. Google Voice lists the greetings you've recorded for use in voicemail.

8. In the Call Presentation section, select the **On** or **Off** radio button. Selecting On turns Call Presentation on, which means you can screen your calls, and people will give their names so you can choose to take their calls or send them to voicemail.

9. Click the **Save Changes** button. Clicking this button brings up the page you see in Figure 10.3.

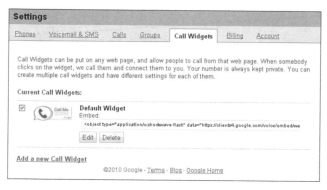

FIGURE 10.3   The Call Widgets embed page.

10. Copy the HTML code from the Embed box. This code is what tells browsers to display your call widget.

11. Embed the HTML code in your own web pages.

Embedding the HTML code in a web page makes the call widget appear on that page. Now anyone who's viewing your page can call you just by clicking the widget.

Solving Access Issues

When you run into problems accessing your account, it's very frustrating. Whether you forget your username or lose your password, you can regain access to Google Voice. Let's take care of those access issues now.

Retrieving Your Username

If you haven't used Google Voice for a while, you might forget the user-name you used when creating your account. Want to recover it? Just follow these steps:

1. Navigate to http://www.google.com/support/voice/ for Google support.

2. Click the **Troubleshooting** link.

3. Click the **Access Issues** link.

4. Click the **Username** link. This opens the page you see in Figure 10.4.

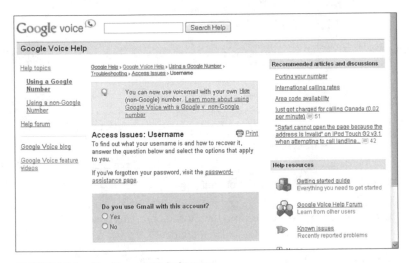

FIGURE 10.4   The Username help page.

5. Follow the directions by clicking the appropriate radio buttons. As you click, other radio buttons appear, depending on your answer, to guide you through the process of recovering your username.

Once you've recovered your username, write it down so you won't forget it again.

Retrieving Your Password

It's pretty easy to forget your password, and people do it all the time. To recover your password, follow these steps:

1. Navigate to http://www.google.com/support/voice/ for Google support.

2. Click the **Troubleshooting** link.

3. Click the **Access Issues** link.

4. Click the **Resetting Your Password** link.

5. Click the **Password-assistance Page** link. This opens the page you see in Figure 10.5.

FIGURE 10.5   The password assistance page.

6. Enter the email address you use for Google Voice. If you don't remember the address, try a few different possibilities—Google Voice tells you if they're invalid.

7. Click the **Submit** button.

Google Voice emails you your password.

Resetting Your Password

There are a couple of reasons why you might want to change your password: You might suspect unauthorized access to your account, or you routinely change it as a security measure. To reset your password, do the following:

1. Navigate to the Google Voice site and log in if necessary.

2. Click the **Settings** link to open the Settings page.

3. Click the **Account** tab.

4. Click the **Google Account Settings** link.

5. Click the **Resetting Your Password** link.

6. Click the **Change Password** link. Clicking the Change Password link opens the page shown in Figure 10.6.

FIGURE 10.6   Changing your password.

7. Enter your current password or security question answer.

8. Type in your new password.

9. Type in the new password again.

10. Click **Save**.

Now that you've changed your password, be sure to remember what the new password is.

Using the Google Voice Troubleshooting Wizard

Google Voice has a troubleshooting wizard that can help you with access problems. When you use this wizard, you answer questions by clicking radio buttons—which makes other radio buttons appear until you arrive (hopefully) at your answer. You'll find the answers to many questions here, such as why you see a "Coming Soon" page when you try to log in to how to change your Google Number.

To give the troubleshooting wizard a try, do this:

1. Navigate to the Google Voice site and log in if necessary.

2. Click the **Help** link.

3. Click the **Troubleshooting** link.

4. Click the **Access Issues** link.

5. Click the **I'm Having Problems with My Account** link. Clicking this link opens the wizard, as shown in Figure 10.7.

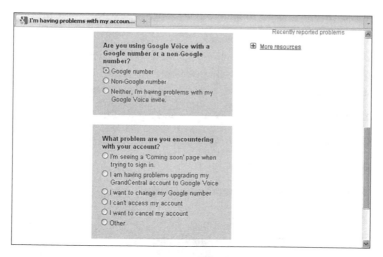

FIGURE 10.7 The Access Issues troubleshooting wizard.

6. Answer the questions asked by the wizard by clicking radio buttons.

The wizard is one of the fastest, most direct ways to get your questions answered.

Changing Your Email Address

If you change your email address, you'll probably also want to change the address associated with your Google Voice account. Unfortunately, this is one thing that's not possible to do. The email account you specified when you set up your account is permanent. There's no way in Google Voice to change that email address—and no way in your Google Account, either.

The only fix: You have to create a new Google Voice account.

Changing Your Username

Want to change you username for any reason? There are two paths here based on whether or not you're using a Gmail account with Google Voice.

If you're using a Gmail account with your Google Voice account, there's no way to change your username (which is your full Gmail account). That's because you can't edit your Gmail account to change your email address. The only fix is to create a new Google Voice account using another email address.

However, if you are using a non-Gmail email account with Google Voice, you can indeed change your username (which is your full email address). Just follow these steps:

1. Navigate to the Google Voice site and log in if necessary.
2. Click the **Settings** link to open the Settings page.
3. Click the **Account** tab.
4. Click the **Google Account Settings** link.
5. Sign in to your account.
6. Click the **Edit** link next to Email Addresses.
7. Enter your new Google Account username.
8. Enter your current password.
9. Click the **Save Email Address** button.

Fixing Voicemail and SMS Issues

You're probably using Google Voice for its voicemail and SMS capabilities. So you need them to work smoothly. What can you do if you have problems with voicemail or SMS? Read on to find out.

Connecting Directly to Voicemail

By default, when you call your Google Voice number, you're asked for your PIN, you have to press the * key, and so on. You can shorten the process by going directly to voicemail. Here's how you do that:

1. Navigate to the Google Voice site and log in if necessary.

2. Click the **Settings** link to open the Settings page.

3. Click the **Phones** tab.

4. Click the **Edit button.**

5. Select the **Show Advanced Settings** link.

6. For each phone from which you want to access your voicemail directly, go to the Voicemail Access section and select **Yes**.

7. Select the correct radio button according to whether you want to enter your PIN when calling your Google number from that phone.

8. Click the **Save** button.

Now you can get your Google Voice voicemail directly from the phones you chose.

You're Not Getting Your SMS Messages

There are many different reasons why you might not be receiving your text messages as you expect—so many, in fact, that Google Voice has created a troubleshooting wizard specifically to resolve problems with receiving SMS messages. To use this wizard and figure out what's wrong with your text messages, follow these steps:

1. Navigate to the Google Voice site and log in if necessary.

2. Click the **Help** link.

3. Click the **Troubleshooting** link.

4. Click the **Call, Voicemail and SMS Issues** link.

5. Click the **SMS Sent to Google Voice Not Being Received** link. Clicking this link opens an SMS troubleshooting wizard, as shown in Figure 10.8.

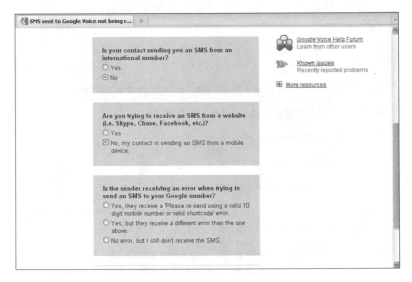

FIGURE 10.8   Troubleshooting wizard for receiving SMS messages.

6. **Follow the directions by clicking the appropriate radio buttons.** As you click, other radio buttons appear, depending on your answers, to guide you through the process of getting your SMS messages.

If you answer the questions accurately, the wizard should help you solve whatever problem you're having with getting text messages.

Others Aren't Receiving Your SMS Messages

If people aren't receiving the text messages you've sent through Google Voice, use the troubleshooting wizard to find and solve the problem; to use the wizard, follow these steps:

1. Navigate to the Google Voice site and log in if necessary.

2. Click the **Help** link.

3. Click the **Troubleshooting** link.

4. Click the **Call, Voicemail and SMS Issues** link.

5. Click the **SMS Sent from Google Voice Not Being Delivered**
   link. Clicking this link opens the SMS troubleshooting wizard
   shown in Figure 10.9.

FIGURE 10.9   Troubleshooting wizard for sending SMS messages.

6. Follow the directions by clicking the appropriate radio buttons.
   As you click, other radio buttons appear, depending on your
   answers, to guide you through the process of sending your SMS
   messages.

By the time you make it to the end of the wizard, you should have the
solution to your problem with sending text messages.

SMS Seems to Come from a 406 Number

When someone sends a text message to your mobile phone without
Google Voice involved at all, the message is listed as coming from that
person's phone number.

When someone sends you a text message from a Google Voice number, the return number is listed as the sender's Google Voice number.

So far, so good.

But when someone sends a text message to your Google Voice number from a non-Google Voice number, the text message appears as though it comes from the 406 area code. What's going on?

It turns out this is the normal way things work—when you are texted at your Google Voice number from a non-Google Voice number, the text message appears to come from a number in the 406 area code. Google sets things up this way so your reply goes through Google Voice and appears to come from your Google Voice number.

So that's why the other person's text message appears to come from the 406 area code—it's so your reply gets routed through Google Voice.

Troubleshooting Call Issues

You might at times experience problems with the calls you make through Google Voice.

For example, you might make a call and get poor call quality. Or you might try to sign up your mobile phone number with Google Voice, only to get an error that tells you that mobile phone number is already in use.

What can you do? Keep reading.

You're Getting Poor Call Quality

As you might expect, call quality can be a big issue when you're using Google Voice. It's possible you'll encounter some of these problems:

- ▶ Inaudible sound
- ▶ Static
- ▶ Echoes
- ▶ Delayed speech
- ▶ Odd sounds

What can you do? You can give Google Voice some feedback so they'll know about the problem. And if you've paid for the call, you can request a refund.

Here's how to give Google Voice feedback on calls you've placed:

1. Navigate to the Google Voice site and log in if necessary.

2. Click the **Placed** link. Clicking the Placed link opens the list of calls you've placed, as shown in Figure 10.10.

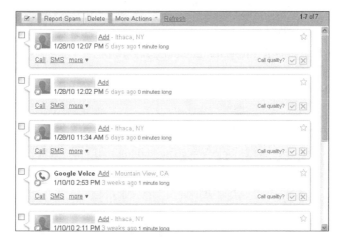

FIGURE 10.10   Google Voice lists the calls you've placed.

3. Find the call you want to give feedback on. You can use the scroll bars to scroll up and down the list if necessary.

4. If you approved of the call quality, click the check mark at right in the call, next to the Call Quality? label.

5. If you did not approve of the call quality, click the X at right in the call, next to the Call Quality? label. Clicking the X opens a drop-down box that itself has a drop-down list box, which you can use to indicate the problem with the call.

   Here are the possible problems listed that you can select:

   ▶ Voice delay

   ▶ Voice echo

- ▶ Could not hear the other person

- ▶ Person could not hear you

- ▶ Call never connected

- ▶ Call got disconnected

- ▶ Low call volume

- ▶ Random sounds

- ▶ Choppy conversation

- ▶ Other

6. Click the **Submit** button in the drop-down box.

Whether positive or negative, your feedback is on its way to Google Voice.

Here's how to give Google Voice feedback on calls you've received:

1. Navigate to the Google Voice site and log in if necessary.

2. Click the **Placed** link. Clicking the Placed link opens the list of calls you've placed, as shown in Figure 10.11.

FIGURE 10.11   Google Voice lists the calls you've received.

3. Locate the call you want to rate. You can use the scroll bars to scroll up and down the list if necessary.

4. If you approved of the call quality, click the check mark at right in the call, next to the Call Quality? label.

5. If you did not approve of the call quality, click the X at right in the call, next to the Call Quality? label. Clicking this icon opens a drop-down box that itself has a drop-down list box, which you can use to indicate the problem with the call. Choose one of the options that best describes the problem you had with the call.

6. Click the **Submit** button in the drop-down box.

Your feedback is now on its way to Google Voice.

When you use Google Voice to make an international call, it costs money. So if you placed an international call that had poor call quality, you might want your money back. In that case, follow these steps:

1. Navigate to the Google Voice site and log in if necessary.

2. Navigate to https://www.google.com/voice/billing/credits. Google Voice lists your most recent international calls that are eligible for refunds.

NOTE

Google Voice makes only short calls available for refunds—the assumption seems to be if you stayed on the phone for a longer call, the call quality was OK.

---

3. Place checks in the checkboxes next to the call(s) you want to get a refund for.

4. Click the **Request Refund** button. Google Voice lets you know via email you'll be receiving a refund.

When you get a refund for a call, you'll see the credit in your Google Voice home page.

Handling Mobile Number Conflicts

When you try to add a mobile number to your Google Voice account—or even when you try to create an account with your mobile number as the primary number—you might receive this error:

This number is already in use as a cell phone on another Google Voice account.

Google Voice says you will get this error only if you have attempted to add a mobile number to more than one Google Voice account. You can't use the same mobile phone number in more than one account at a time.

The only fix is to remove that mobile phone number from your other Google Voice account.

Google Voice admits that in the past, you may have cancelled a previous account and that the mobile phone number associated with that account might not be freed up. They now say that you will be prompted to free that number when you try to add it to a different account.

You Can't See All Your Numbers

Say you've told Google Voice about several different phones—but when you make a call from the website (for example, using the Call button), only one possible phone number appears. What's going on?

It turns out that you've probably selected the Remember My Choice checkbox when you made your previous call. When you check that checkbox, Google Voice displays only the number of the phone you're using to place that call, and will also display that number as the only option next time.

The fix? Make another call from the phone Google Voice tells you about—and in the dialog box that opens when you place the call, uncheck the Remember My Choice checkbox. The next time you make a call, all your phones should be listed.

Your Call Can't Be Completed as Dialed

Sometimes, the calls you make can't be completed as dialed—even though you know you dialed a working number.

This is a more common issue than you might think. There can be all kinds of reasons for it, such as the recipient of the call may have blocked you or you need to dial a 1 before dialing the number. This is such a common problem that Google Voice has created a wizard for it, and you can access that wizard this way:

1. Navigate to the Google Voice site and log in if necessary.

2. Click the **Help** link.

3. Click the **Troubleshooting** link.

4. Click the **Call, Voicemail and SMS Issues** link.

5. Click the **Call Cannot Be Connected as Dialed** link. Clicking this link opens a troubleshooting wizard, as shown in Figure 10.12.

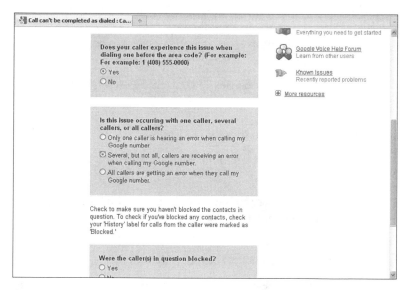

FIGURE 10.12   A troubleshooting wizard for nonconnected calls.

6. Follow the directions by clicking the appropriate radio buttons. As you click, other radio buttons appear, depending on your answers, to guide you through the process of getting your calls connected.

There are plenty of reasons calls can't be connected—and most of them don't have anything to do with Google Voice—so be prepared to ask for help from the phone company of the person you're calling or who's calling you.

Posting to the Help Forum

If you can't find help for your issue, try the Google Voice help forum— posting your question there often gets quick answers. Here's how to post a question:

1. Navigate to the Google Voice site and log in if necessary.

2. Click the **Help** link.

3. Click the **Help Forum** link.

4. Click the **Problem Solving** link.

5. Scan the list of articles to see if your question has been addressed. If so, click the topic you'd like to read about.

6. To post your issue to the Help Forum, click **Post a Question**.

7. Enter your username.

8. Read the terms of service.

9. Click the **Accept and Continue** button. Google Voice displays a new web page.

10. Select a category for your question from the **Which Category Best Describes Your Question?** list box. The default is Problem Solving.

11. Enter your question in the **Your Question** text box.

12. Click the **Continue** button. Google Voice displays a new web page with possible answers to your question.

13. If your answer appears on this page, click the **I Found My Answer** button.

14. If you did not find your answer, click the **Continue** button. Google Voice opens a new web page.

15. Enter the text of your question in the **Tell Us More About Your Question** text box.

16. If you want to be notified when people reply to your question, check the **Email Me When People Reply** checkbox.

17. Click the **Post Question** button.

Your question will be posted to the Help Forum, and you can check the Forum from time to time to see if anyone has answered it. (On the Help Forum, the number of answers appears next to the link to your question title.)

Emailing Google Voice

Is it possible to simply email Google Voice about your problem?

Yes. It's a little-known fact, but you can email Google Voice. If your issue is handled in a help topic, you probably won't get an answer. But it is possible to email the Google Voice team, as you can see from the web page in Figure 10.13.

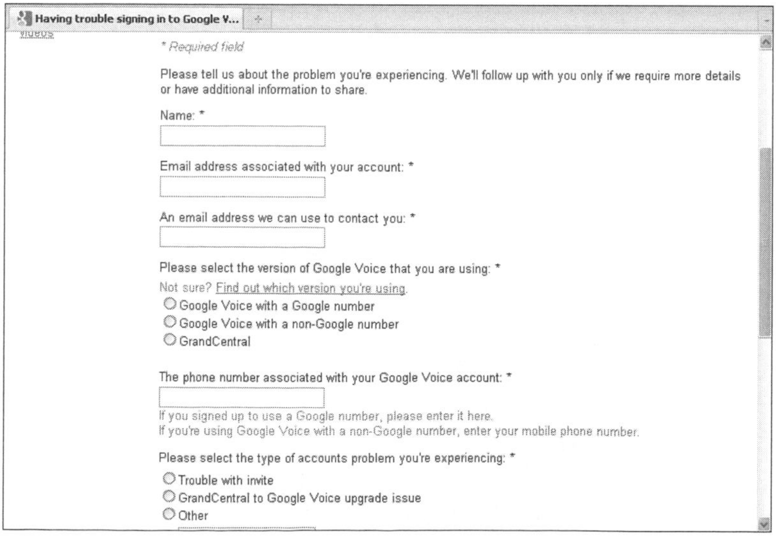

FIGURE 10.13 Emailing Google Voice.

How do you email Google Voice about a problem? All the troubleshooting wizards (those pages that display more radio buttons as you click other radio buttons) eventually let you email the Google Voice team if the wizard can't answer your question. So if you really want to email Google Voice, just find a troubleshooting wizard and keep clicking radio buttons until it gives you the chance to email the support team.

Summary

Overall, Google Voice is reliable and easy to use. But when problems arise, you now know how to deal with them. Enjoy the many benefits of Google Voice—customization, flexibility, and affordability. Happy calling!

Index

T

temporary call forwarding, 14, 77-78, 141-142

text messages
406 area code, 131-132
blocking, 132-133
explained, 15-16, 119
forwarding to email, 127-129
international SMS, 130-131
organizing, 126-127
receiving, 125-126
replying to, 124-125
reporting as spam, 133-134
sending, 119
to contacts, 121-122
from Google Voice mobile site, 152
by replying to voicemail, 122-124
with SMS button, 120
setting email address for, 129-130
troubleshooting
text messages from 406 area code, 131-132, 187-188
text messages not received by others, 186-187
text messages not received by you, 185-186
voicemail notification with, 142-143

transcripts (voicemail)
explained, 11
receiving, 85-86
turning off, 101

Treat as Spam option, 81

troubleshooting
access issues, 179
changing email address, 184
changing username, 184

resetting passwords, 181-182
retrieving passwords, 181
retrieving username, 180
with troubleshooting wizard, 183-184
call issues
call cannot be completed as dialed, 192-194
inability to see numbers, 192
mobile number conflicts, 192
poor call quality, 188-191
creating call widgets, 177-179
emailing Google Voice, 195-196
invitations, 26-27
posting to Help Forum, 194-195
text messages
text messages from 406 area code, 131-132, 187-188
text messages not received by others, 186-187
text messages not received by you, 185-186
voicemail, 185

Troubleshooting link, 180

turning on/off
Call Presentation, 10
calls, 143
Do Not Disturb, 81-82
voicemail transcriptions, 101

U

Unblock Caller link, 133
Unread button, 88
unwanted calls, avoiding, 78
blocking specific callers, 79-80
Do Not Disturb feature, 81-82, 155
labeling calls as spam, 81
setting ring schedule, 78

unwanted text messages, blocking,
132-133
Upload dialog box, 61
uploading photos, 61-63
Username link, 180
usernames
  changing, 184
  retrieving, 180

V

Verify button, 89
voicemail
  connecting directly to, 185
  downloading, 99
  emailing, 98
  embedding in Web pages, 100
  explained, 83
  for existing mobile numbers, 11
  greetings
    *making recorded greetings
    active, 94*
    recording, 92-94
    *selecting which greeting to play
    by caller, 95-96*
  listening as callers record voicemail, 13
  listening to, 86-87
  notes, 96-97
  on mobile phones, 83-85
  organizing, 87-88
  receiving on phone
    *connecting directly to voicemail,
    91-92*
    PINs, 90-91
  receiving on Web, 153
    listening to voicemail, 86-87
    organizing voicemail, 87-88

*sending voicemail notifications
  to different email address,
  88-89*
voicemail transcripts, 85-86
replying to with text messages,
122-124
sending all calls to, 100-101
transcripts
  explained, 11
  receiving, 85-86
  turning off, 101
troubleshooting, 185
voicemail notification with SMS,
142-143
Voicemail & SMS tab (Settings
page), 7
Voicemail link, 85

W-X-Y-Z

Web
  embedding voicemail in, 100
  making international calls from,
  160-163
  receiving voicemail on, 85
    listening to voicemail, 86-87
    organizing voicemail, 87-88
    *sending voicemail notifications
    to different email address,
    88-89*
    voicemail transcripts, 85-86
widgets, call widgets
  creating, 177-179
  explained, 17-18
wizards, Google Voice troubleshooting wizard, 183-184
Word Verification section (Google
accounts), 30
Yes, Suggest This Picture button, 63

Sams**TeachYourself**

from Sams Publishing

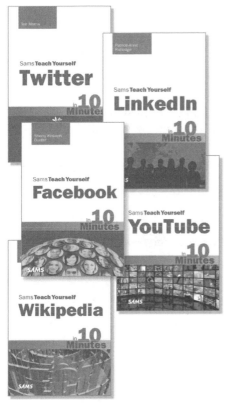

Sams **Teach Yourself in 10 Minutes** offers straightforward, practical answers for fast results.

These small books of 250 pages or less offer tips that point out shortcuts and solutions, cautions that help you avoid common pitfalls, notes that explain additional concepts, and provide additional information. By working through the 10-minute lessons, you learn everything you need to know quickly and easily!

When you only have time for the answers, Sams Teach Yourself books are your best solution.

Visit **informit.com/samsteachyourself** for a complete listing of the products available.

FREE Online Edition

Your purchase of **Sams Teach Yourself Google Voice in 10 Minutes** includes access to a free online edition for 45 days through the Safari Books Online subscription service. Nearly every Sams book is available online through Safari Books Online, along with more than 5,000 other technical books and videos from publishers such as Addison-Wesley Professional, Cisco Press, Exam Cram, IBM Press, O'Reilly, Prentice Hall, and Que.

SAFARI BOOKS ONLINE allows you to search for a specific answer, cut and paste code, download chapters, and stay current with emerging technologies.

Activate your FREE Online Edition at www.informit.com/safarifree

> **STEP 1:** Enter the coupon code: DBZSOXA.

> **STEP 2:** New Safari users, complete the brief registration form. Safari subscribers, just log in.

If you have difficulty registering on Safari or accessing the online edition, please e-mail customer-service@safaribooksonline.com